HEARTBEAT OF THE UNIVERSITY

The Founders Series

HEARTBEAT OF THE UNIVERSITY

125 Years of Purdue Bands

By JOHN NORBERG with contributions by KATHY MATTER

PURDUE UNIVERSITY PRESS
West Lafayette, Indiana

Library of Congress Cataloging-in-Publication Data

Norberg, John.
Heartbeat of the university : 125 years of Purdue bands / by John Norberg.
p. cm. -- (Founders series)
Includes index.
ISBN 978-1-55753-596-2
1. Purdue University--Bands--History. 2. Bands (Music)--Indiana--West Lafayette--History. I. Title. II. Series.

ML28.W47P874 2011
784.8'306077295--dc22

2011011265

Photography:
JC Allen and Son • Joel Benson • Suzie Coles • Wayne Doebling • Group Photos Inc. • Gavin Jones • Max Jones • *Lafayette Journal and Courier* • Kathy Matter • Jesse McGreevy • George Munro • Purdue Photographic Services • Purdue University Libraries, Karnes Archives and Special Collections • Brent Russell • Scott Sermersheim • Sara Suppinger • Warren Photo • Joe Winters

Cartoonists:
William B. Robinson *(Indianapolis News)* • David Sattler • Gaar Williams *(Chicago Tribune)*

Photo scanning and restoration:
Jason Gary • Mary Jane Gavenda • Tracy Matz

Book and cover design:
Mary Jane Gavenda

This book celebrates 125 years of the Purdue Bands and Orchestras. With ensembles representing a vast array of musical types, not to mention the celebrated "All-American" Marching Band and the "World's Largest Drum," Purdue Bands has been an integral part of the fabric of our University. They are visible at Purdue events and games, helping alumni and friends get in the Boilermaker spirit.

But the Purdue Bands represent much more than collegiate music at its finest. Members are also accomplished Purdue students, nearly three-quarters of who have majors related to math or science, although nearly every major is represented within the ensembles. They hail from hometowns across the country and around the world.

One of my fondest gameday activities is spending time on the field with our "All-American" Band's feature twirlers, including the Golden Girl, Girl in Black, the Silver Twins and Miss Boilerette. With all the flash and celebration of a college home game, the twirlers serve as leaders of the "All-American" Marching Band as well as ambassadors for Purdue University.

I appreciate the vibrant and dynamic role the Purdue Bands and Orchestras have played at Purdue. They offer valuable leadership roles for members and activities that broaden the student experience beyond our classrooms and laboratories.

Whether you are a fan of jazz, percussion, string orchestra, or concert band music, the Purdue Bands and Orchestras has something for everyone. They have contributed so much to the University's history and continue to help us celebrate our heritage, our successes and our Boilermaker spirit.

Thank you to the members of the Purdue Bands and Orchestras for helping make Purdue proud for 125 years. I know you will continue your good work for generations to come.

Hail Purdue!

— France A. Córdova, President

Jay S. Gephart, Director of Bands, Director AAMB, Wind Ensemble

I am deeply honored to hold the position of Director of Bands at Purdue University as we celebrate a significant milestone in the organization's history—our 125th anniversary in 2011. Throughout these 125 years, Purdue band traditions have been the fabric by which we knit ourselves together, from one era to another. Perhaps that is why I so enjoy being part of the Purdue Bands and Orchestras family. Everyone whose lives have been touched by this department takes enormous pride in the fact that these beloved traditions have endured the test of time and are as important to the entire Boilermaker nation today as they were when they were created decades ago.

In the pages of this book, we tell our story and celebrate 125 years of this amazing program. This is a story of music making, of friendships that last a lifetime, of changed lives, and of school spirit and Boilermaker pride. Each chapter and photograph gives the reader a glimpse into the lives of the countless men and women who are members of the Purdue band family. As you read our story, you can almost hear these words from "Hail Purdue" leap from the pages:

Ever grateful, ever true,
Thus we raise our song anew;
Of the days we've spent with you,
All hail our own Purdue!

The best part is that the history of Purdue Bands does not end with this book. History is being made with each passing year and will continue for decades to come. Our most important legacy, of course, continues to be our students. They are the driving force behind excellence and are the inspiration to the Purdue community, past and present. I look forward to creating, with them, the next chapter in Purdue band history!

— Jay S. Gephart

PURDUE

TABLE OF CONTENTS

Purdue University campus scene from the 1880s, the decade of Purdue Bands' inception.

CHAPTER ONE

THE BEGINNING

Previous page: The Purdue military band escorts a Lafayette military company starting off for the Spanish–American War in 1898.

Their caps turned backward celebrating victory, members of the "All-American" Marching Band strut and swagger as they play for old Purdue.

Filing out of Ross-Ade Stadium, their home field where they thrill cheering crowds with halftime shows no other band on earth can do, they march in seventy-five ranks of five, forming a line that is more than a football field long.

If they marched in single file, four feet apart, their line would stretch longer than the height of the tallest building in America.

The 375 musicians and auxiliary unit members dressed in black, gold, and white sway their instruments, flags, and batons left and right, blasting "Hail Purdue" while Boilermakers line the streets clapping and singing to a melody that's sweet to their ears and warm to their hearts.

The "All-American" Marching Band is the heartbeat of Purdue University, pounding like a big bass drum, reverberating across the campus, and building Boilermaker spirit wherever it is seen and heard.

Pointing their instruments upward—confident and proud—while keeping pace to a fast marching beat, each band section adds the harmony that all blends together in the familiar melody.

The Golden Girl leads the parade, followed by the Girl in Black, the Silver Twins, the Goldusters, the Golden Silks Color Guard, and the drum majors. Behind them march the musicians including seventy trumpets, forty trombones, thirty baritone horns and mellophones, fifty tenor and alto saxophones, forty clarinets, and twenty piccolos. In the middle of it all are twenty-one big sousaphones and thirty-eight drummers beating basses, cymbals, snares, and tenors.

Standing at the front and to the side, Purdue's Director of Bands Jay Gephart looks back and is overwhelmed by the enormous column of musicians, marching in step, shouting with enthusiasm, cheering, and performing. Whistles blow up and down the long columns. The drum line beats a fast roll that all the musicians recognize and on signal, stretching more than one hundred yards, the band plays.

"To your call once more we rally
Alma Mater, hear our praise
Where the Wabash spreads its valley
Filled with joy our voices raise
From the skies in swelling echoes
Come the cheers that tell the tale
Of your vic'tries and your heroes
Hail Purdue! We sing all hail!"

This band is the pride of Purdue and there's no mistaking it as the collegiate musicians march down the street attracting a crowd wherever they go. They say that when they cheer the earth will tremble and they are known throughout the land as the best in marching music.

They're the Boilermaker band.

"Hail, Hail to Old Purdue
All hail to our old gold and black
Hail, Hail to Old Purdue
Our friendship may she never lack
Ever grateful, ever true
Thus we raise our song anew
Of the days we've spent with you
All hail our own Purdue!"

Every time something good happens at the University, people want the "All-American" band to lead the celebration with "Hail Purdue."

And the band is always there to play it, in arenas and in concert halls, in the sun, rain, and snow, and at times even when others have already gone home. The band is always there.

At a university without a College of Music, this is an internationally famous musical organization that has made a huge mark on the history of American marching bands.

The Purdue band was first in the nation to break out of military ranks and form a letter on the football field. The Block "P," first formed in 1907, is still created before each home football game.

And in November of 2010, as it launched a year-long celebration of its 125th anniversary, the Purdue "All-American" Marching Band became the first Big Ten unit to march through Herald Square and the streets of New York City leading the Macy's Thanksgiving Day Parade.

Forty million people watched on television and many millions more lined the streets as the band played "Hail Purdue," "Strike Up the Band," and "New York, New York."

The band members cheered, high stepped, low stepped, used a run-on step, bent backward, leaned forward, and did kick-steps that lifted them off the street as they marched along the 2.65 mile parade route, capturing the hearts of America with their sound, spirit, and enthusiasm.

It was a crowning moment in Purdue history and one that was shared with generations of Boilermakers who have built the great traditions of this "All-American" Marching Band.

How did it all begin? How did it all come to this? Where in the great history of Purdue did this band get its start? How did it grow to be among the biggest and best in the world? Where did it get its "All-American" name and the traditions that are now part of University lore?

Like a band marching in a parade, it happened one step at a time. And there were some very classy steps along the way.

Purdue University marks 1869 as its founding. When it opened for the first day of classes on September 16, 1874, there were only three buildings, six instructors, and thirty-nine students.

The University was located on the outskirts of the small town of Chauncey, which had petitioned in 1871 to be annexed by the growing city of Lafayette across the Wabash River. However, the petition was denied and in 1888 Chauncey became West Lafayette.

The campus grew slowly but steadily on treeless land. University Hall, which still stands today, was finished in 1877. The Science Building and Boarding Hall (also known as Ladies Hall) emerged along with a men's dormitory called Purdue Hall as well as Military Hall and the Gymnasium—all of red brick. Agricultural Hall went up along with Mechanics Hall.

Amidst this handful of buildings on the barren landscape, musicians formed the first Purdue University Band in the fall of 1886.

As a land-grant university, Purdue was charged with teaching agriculture, the mechanical arts, and providing military training to all male students. The band started with a cadet drum corps for the Purdue Student Army Training Corps—a predecessor of ROTC.

Throughout history, armies used drummers and other musicians to beat a marching cadence, to lead troops in drill and into battles. Marching bands played a significant role in army life during the Civil War, which had ended just four years before Purdue was founded.

But by the fall of 1886 the cadet drum corps had expanded to something much more. Community bands that played in town and city parks were popular throughout Indiana and the nation, and some of the students who arrived to study at Purdue in those early days came with trumpets, clarinets, trombones, and a love for music that would not be denied.

BAND FIRSTS

First in the nation to break out of military ranks and form a letter on the football field.

First to carry all the colors of the Big Ten schools.

First to play the opposing school's fight song.

First to think enormously when it came to drums, creating the "World's Largest Drum."

First to become an annual part of the Indianapolis 500 starting in 1919.

First to stage a night halftime show on a completely darkened field by illuminating its members and instruments with tiny, battery-operated strings of lights.

First to create nationwide recognition for its featured twirlers: the Golden Girl, the Girl in Black, and the Silver Twins.

First to have an alumnus on the moon —Neil Armstrong in 1969.

First to be invited by the Ministry of Culture to perform in Beijing, China.

First Big Ten band to march in the Macy's Thanksgiving Day Parade.

John Lankin, student director in 1899.

Purdue students started Purdue bands.

The overwhelming majority of these students didn't learn their music in school. They learned from their mothers, fathers, uncles, and neighbors.

People have always loved music, and in nineteenth century rural America, when most families could not travel to the great concert halls to hear performances, they found another way to entertain themselves. They made music themselves.

Band music was attracting a huge national following. In the mid-1880s John Philip Sousa was gaining international acclaim for his marches. In 1889 his composition, "The Washington Post," was first performed.

Given the era and the human need and love for music, it is impossible to imagine that a band wouldn't emerge on the young Purdue campus.

And so it did.

In October of 1886, almost a year after the student newspaper noted the purchase of a bugle, the same paper noted that the band "as thus far organized consists of Floyd and Lutz, cornets; Hicks, baritone; Remster, alto; Butterworth, tuba."

From those five musicians attached to military training came the Purdue University Bands and one of the world's largest—and best—marching band units.

It was a fitting year to start a band program at Purdue. P. T. Barnum's "Greatest Show On Earth" rolled down Main Street in Lafayette on July 28, 1886. That same year there was a two-mile long parade of Civil War veterans in town. Patriotism and showmanship—two elements of the band that would survive the nineteenth century and carry through to the twenty-first century—were running high.

But the cadet drum corps, as it was called in those early years, probably played sporadically. Drilling itself was sporadic on the young campus, depending on whether or not someone qualified to conduct the exercises was on staff.

Football was introduced to Purdue in 1887, and it didn't take the students long to notice the natural affinity between the sport and bands.

The band's early days depended greatly on the talent that was enrolled at Purdue. In 1894 the band lacked a snare drummer until Louis Bianci signed on.

From its simple start in 1886, the unit had grown slightly by 1895 when Lieutenant S. W. Miller, 5th U.S. Infantry, reorganized the military band, supported with contributions from faculty and students.

On October 10, 1895, the Purdue student newspaper, the *Exponent*, noted, as if in encouragement, "There is a fine band in view." This newly reorganized band made its first public appearance in 1896 at the head of cadet battalions.

It was the year Sousa introduced "The Stars and Stripes Forever."

Band reorganization was frequent in those early days at Purdue when there was no permanent director. Directors, who were professors or students, came and went and were elected by the band members.

In 1896 the Purdue student yearbook, the *Debris*, pictured a thirteen-member band. Its members were dressed in military uniforms that had changed little from the days of the Civil War—dark suits, probably black or blue, with gold braids and flat-topped caps. As usual, members of the band were required to furnish their own uniforms, their own instruments, sheet music, and maintenance funds.

Included in the photo are a snare drum and a bass drum, cornets, a solo and first alto, a clarinet, a slide trombone, drummers, and a drum major named F. A. Compton, class of 1899. The director was W. D. Rudy, class of 1899.

During the 1899-1900 school years, the band, now under the direction of J. L. Larkin, began to attract attention at athletic events—football and baseball. The 1900 *Debris* said,

The oldest existing photograph of the band depicts members in 1896.

"No organization in Purdue has received more worthy praise this year than the University Band. It has labored under difficulties all year, but, having reached an unusual degree of efficiency, it can now be classed foremost among the best college bands in the country."

The Purdue *Exponent* said:

> *Nothing tends more to develop in the students that keen sense of loyalty to Purdue than the band. Good college bands are such a rarity that the students in enumerating the many good things of Purdue are pleased to give this organization a prominent place on the list. The band this year is far superior to any at any previous time, and it has received many compliments for its excellent musical entertainments given at different times in Lafayette.*
>
> *The members have shown their loyalty to the University by furnishing music at all of the football and baseball games without compensation for their services. The repertoire of music of the band consists of some of the best standard overtures and marches. Besides the admirable feature that each member is an individual musician, there exists that unison and harmony which is necessary to the success of any musical organization.*

During the 1900-1901 school year, G. A. Young, who would become head of the School of Mechanical Engineering, became director. Young continued as director in 1902, when as a result of his efforts, band membership increased to fifty—the first big jump in the size of the organization. Also under Young, the band moved toward solving its financial problems by becoming partially self-supporting through revenue derived from concerts and other appearances.

The addition of new men did not simply increase the numbers of the band. New instruments had been added, providing depth and richness to the sound—more B-flat cornets were included, more clarinets were featured. One young man played the saxophone, another a ballad horn. There was a bass trombone and a valve trombone. There were more drummers, a cymbal player, bass players, and young men playing the piccolo.

There were more officers. In addition to electing a student director, the band members also elected students to the positions of manager, president, and secretary-treasurer.

It continued as a military band, with the student receiving military training credit for playing their instruments. In fact, Purdue male students were required to have two years of military training at Purdue until 1965, and performing in the band always fulfilled that obligation.

The Purdue band, 1898.

Spring review of 1896.

Group photo, 1899–1900.

On October 31, 1903—Halloween—the band and the entire community were in a festive mood. The Purdue versus Indiana University football game was that day, and for the first time it would be played in Indianapolis at the new Washington Park Stadium. So many people planned to attend the game that two special trains were brought into Lafayette to carry everyone south.

Trains were the only reasonable way to make the journey, the only mode of transportation at the time that could reach Indianapolis within a few hours, making the one day round-trip possible.

That Saturday morning before the big game the *Lafayette Courier* streamed a headline across the top of page one: "Rah, rah, rah, rah, rah, rah, rah, rah, rah! Purdue!"—nine "rahs" in all. "Great Gridiron Struggle today," the headline continued.

"Lafayette will send an immense delegation to Indianapolis to witness the contest," the newspaper reported. "Admirers of the old gold and black are sanguine that the crimson and white banners of the Bloomington boys will be trailed in the dust of the Hoosier capital before the sun sets."

But instead, the sun set that day on the greatest tragedy in the history of Purdue.

One train of fourteen cars was already filled by 7:30 that morning. The first car carried team members and a few special guests. The second car carried the band and other guests. Fan cars followed.

At 9:45 a.m., just minutes from its destination, the lead train that held the team, band, and fans rounded a curve and crashed into a ten-section group of coal cars being switched from a siding.

Seventeen people died, thirteen of them members of the football team, and more than forty people were seriously injured. Twenty-nine members of the football team in the lead car were hospitalized. The car they were in was shattered.

The second car carrying the band tumbled off the tracks and into a gravel pit. The seats came loose and all the passengers were thrown to the back of the car. The car stopped on an embankment with one end up by the tracks and the other at the bottom of the hill.

Newspapers listed injuries such as crushed legs, broken arms, bruises, mashed hands, head cuts, and worse.

No band members were killed or seriously injured, but the *Lafayette Courier* carried this account from band member L. M. Kelsey:

> *There were about 30 girls in the second car and a few others including Professor Alford, Professor Turner and Miss Caroline Fahnestock. We did not have a moment's warning and when the car went to the left over the bank, we were all thrown in a mass. The fellows on top began to pass seats out of the windows so that we could get out. A fellow with his face covered with blood and dirt was the first one out and he began helping the girls out.*
>
> *I was one of the first out and I said to him, "Get away from here. If the girls see you they'll faint." I don't know just how we got out, but we climbed out of the windows, I remember, because the door couldn't be reached.*
>
> *The car wasn't damaged much and I only saw one girl hurt, Miss Lita Smith of this city. Not one of the band members was injured, but some of us lost our coats and instruments. The girls acted all right until they got on their feet on the outside. Then whenever a piece of glass would fall or a little noise was made they would go into hysterics. We got them away from there as fast as we could.*

The train wreck of 1903.

In 1904 Emrick joined the band as a freshman. He is believed to be the clarinetist sixth from the left in the second row.

Other accounts told the stories of women and men heroically using articles of clothing or other found items to bandage injured people scattered among the horrific chaos of blood, bodies, and debris.

The game was never played, and a decision was made to build a gymnasium to honor those who died in the tragedy. Ground was broken on May 30, 1908. The facility cost $85,000, with $25,000 coming from the University, $15,000 from the New York Central Railroad, $2,500 from Purdue alumnus and benefactor George Ade, and the rest from small contributions.

It was named Memorial Gymnasium, which still stands on the campus, and was dedicated on May 19, 1909. The Purdue Band would play there many times, adding spirit to Boilermaker basketball games.

It was into this atmosphere that Paul Spotts Emrick entered his freshman year in 1904. He was listed in the *Debris* that year as a clarinetist. His name was at the top of the list, which was not arranged alphabetically.

He very probably was not only the best clarinetist in the band, but also the very best musician. Having already directed a band before coming to Purdue, and coming from a family of band directors, he probably assumed a leadership role very shortly after blowing his first note on the campus.

Destiny had big things in store for him. Out of this young man from Fulton County, Indiana, emerged the Purdue "All-American" Marching Band and eventually symphony orchestras, concert bands, and even jazz bands.

CHAPTER TWO

THE MILITARY YEARS

The Creative Genius of Paul Spotts Emrick

Previous page: An animated Paul Spotts Emrick directs the band in the late 1940s.

Emrick at his desk in the Armory, circa 1930s.

Paul Spotts Emrick was a man who savored the limelight, and on October 5, 1935, he glowed with satisfaction as he listened to applause coming from all around him.

The Purdue University military band he had directed for all but one of the past thirty years was standing at attention in the middle of what was then named Dyche Stadium in Evanston, Illinois. The sound of his band boys' music still echoed through the curved grandstands in the facility during the seconds before the cheering began.

It was the end of halftime during the first Big Ten football game ever played at night. The stadium lights had been turned off for the band show, and it was pitch black in the stands packed with thirty thousand people who had come to see Purdue and Northwestern University play.

The only lights during the halftime show came from the field, from the Purdue band itself. Headlights shone from inside the big bass drum. A drum major stood in front of it, fire pouring off the ends of his flaming baton. White lights on the plumes of the marchers' hats sparkled in the darkness and colored lights lined their instruments.

An electrical engineer by profession and a bandleader at heart, Emrick had just completed a halftime light show reminiscent of an Independence Day celebration. There had never before been a lighted halftime band show anywhere, and the spectators were standing and responding to each surprise as though they were watching fireworks, screaming "Ooohhh . . . aaahhh."

The press box that evening was packed with reporters who were in Chicago from all over the country to cover the Cubs and Detroit Tigers playing at Wrigley Field in the World Series. This Purdue versus Northwestern game was an extra assignment, something to do in the evening.

Among those reporters was a radio broadcaster as well as a sportscaster with a smooth voice that was better known to millions of people all across the country than the voice of their next-door neighbors. He laid the foundation for modern sports announcing. His name was Ted Husing, and he was announcing the game for CBS that night.

He was well known and loved by listeners. He could also be controversial and made enemies. He was banned from broadcasting Harvard University games for two years after he called their quarterback's performance "putrid." Baseball Commissioner Kenesaw Mountain Landis banned him from doing play-by-play at the World Series after he criticized umpires in 1934.

In 1935 at the height of his fame, Husing was broadcasting the Purdue versus Northwestern game; the Boilermakers would win, 7-0. As he watched the halftime show that night, Husing thought about the title given to the greatest college football players in the country. They were "All-America" or "All-American" players, and after particularly great performances, announcers would often say, "That young man is a real 'All-American.'"

When Emrick's Purdue band finished playing that night, Husing made a statement on the CBS network radio to a national audience that had lasting impact. "This," he said, "is a real 'All-American' band."

Standing on the field, accepting the last of the applause, and marching his boys to the sidelines, Emrick didn't hear what Husing said that night. He would learn about it later. However, people all over the country heard it live, and back home in Indiana, people thought the name was perfect—a nickname that could not be improved. It stuck.

From that moment on, unofficially at first but eventually as a formal name, the Purdue University Military Band became the Purdue University "All-American" Marching Band, and it was led by an "All-American" director.

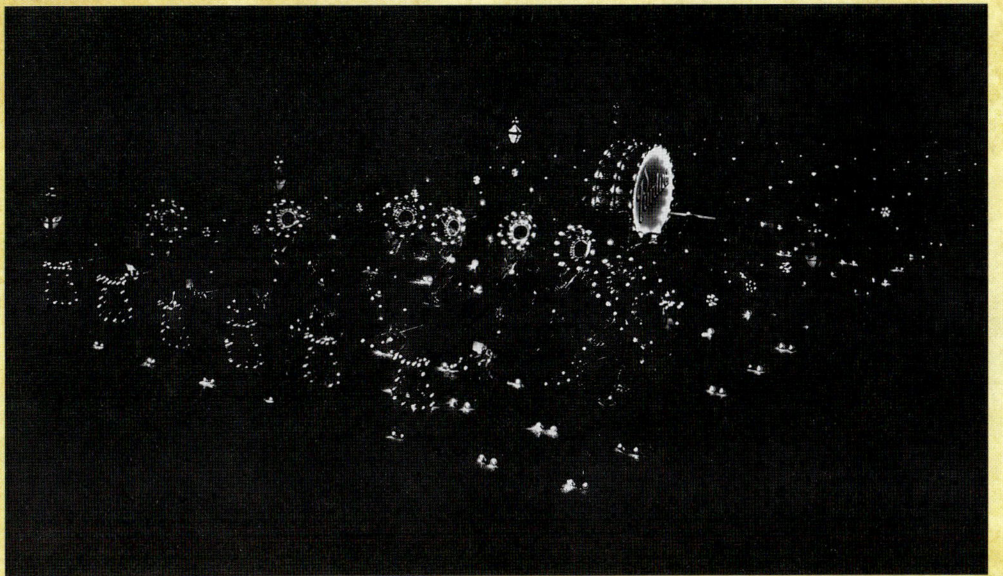

Let there be lights!

Emrick's background as an electrical engineer combined with his sense of showmanship produced the first illuminated halftime show for a game between Purdue and Northwestern at Evanston on October 5, 1935 *(upper left)*.

Purdue gave several illuminated shows later and used the Block "P" and the Purdue letters *(lower left)*. The band won first place in the Kentucky Derby Parade in 1935 with their illuminated show. The trophy is displayed in a birdcage atop the "World's Largest Drum" *(upper right)*.

Facing page: Fans enjoy the band perform from the stands and their cars on Stewart Field in 1912. Elliott Hall was later built on Stewart Field.

The Purdue band appeared at the dedication of the Victory Arch in Indianapolis in 1919, welcoming soldiers home from World War I.

Paul Spotts Emrick was born in Rochester, Indiana, in 1884—two years before the Purdue band was organized. He himself was only two years old when he sat on a stool and listened to the Rochester Citizens Band at practice playing "When Johnny Comes Marching Home Again," "Rally 'Round the Flag," and "John Brown's Body."

He was born to Levi and Sarah Alice Spotts Emrick. The boy got his middle name, Spotts, from his mother's maiden name, and it became his lifelong nickname.

Levi Emrick played the baritone horn in the Rochester Citizens Band alongside his brother-in-law, Ovid Osgood, who played the cornet.

On July 14, 1888, having suffered from tuberculosis for several months, Levi Emrick died at the age of forty. He left his wife and two children, one of them Paul, age four.

After the death of his father and under the wing of his Uncle Ovid Osgood, Emrick was anxious to play a musical instrument, and the Rochester Citizens Band members helped teach him. He had natural talent and an enthusiasm for band music.

As a high school student, Emrick directed musical groups that played for dances and dramatic productions. He was involved in summer band concerts and other events that featured music.

A 1902 photo of the Rochester Citizens Band shows Emrick sitting in the front row, holding a clarinet. He could also play the violin, the cornet, and several other instruments. In fact, he was so versatile that years later his band students would each have a different impression about what was his primary instrument.

It was the clarinet.

When Emrick enrolled at Purdue, one of his first steps was to enter the military band. There were thirty-nine musicians in the band that year. The next year, in 1905, when Emrick was elected president and director, there were forty-five members. Among his first goals was to make the band the largest in the Western Athletic Conference (now the Big Ten).

The size of the band in the first years after the turn of the century seems small in comparison with today's standards, but at the time there were just more than one thousand students enrolled at Purdue. A band membership of thirty-five represented almost 4 percent of the entire student body. If 4 percent of the forty thousand students enrolled at Purdue in 2011 marched in the band, there would be about 1,600 musicians on the field at football halftimes.

Emrick was reelected director of the band during his junior and senior years. In 1907 he and the Purdue band established the first of many firsts for any college band. In that day it was common for bands to march onto a football field during halftime. The band would stop and play, always remaining in straight rows.

However, Emrick added a new dimension. To the total surprise of spectators at the football games, he had the band break its ranks and form the letter "P." That move, a first in American marching band history, opened the doors to the creativity seen in band shows today.

Like many of his ideas, it was one that dates back to his family in Rochester and his boyhood spent at a cottage on Lake Manitou. "Most ideas come from nature," he said in an interview with the *Lafayette Journal and Courier* in the fall of 1953 as he neared his retirement.

As a boy, he said, he had watched wild geese fly over the lake in the fall. "Usually, they'd fly in a 'V,'" he continued. "But once in a while, they'd change formation and fly in various figures. I used to wonder if you could do that with men drilling."

Emrick graduated in 1908 with a degree in electrical engineering, and he took a job as an electrical engineer with a traction company in South Bend the day after his graduation.

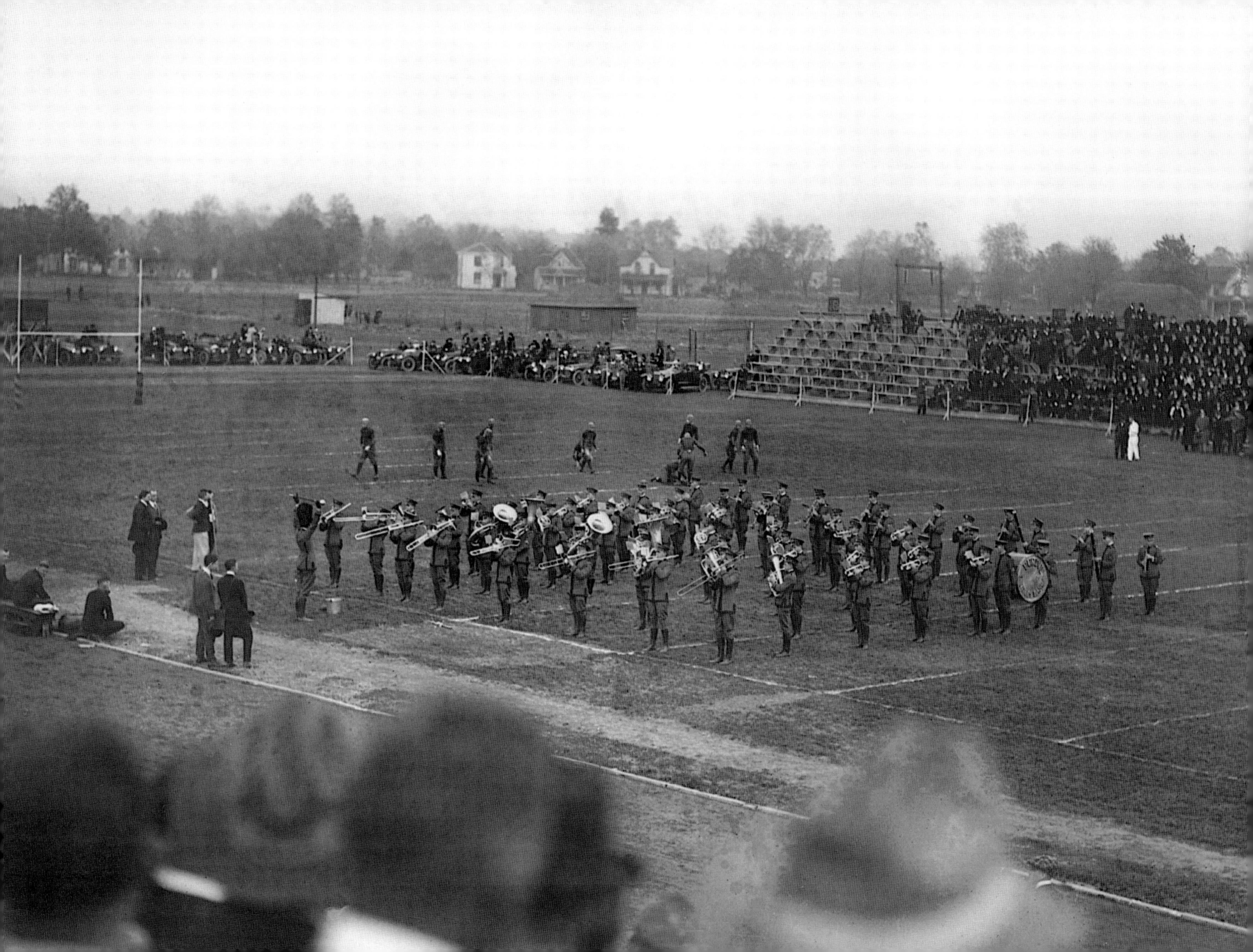

One of the first iterations of the Block "P" formation in 1922.

Facing page: Band shows off new "World's Largest Drum" in downtown Indianapolis in September 1921.

It didn't last long. The following fall he returned to Purdue to teach electrical engineering, which was his official duty until 1938, but his heart and much of his energy were devoted to the band.

As it always would be under Emrick, the band was structured under military guidelines. In 1912 he was listed as conductor and major in the band. There were a captain, lieutenants, sergeants, and corporals. To Emrick, the precision of a marching band and the discipline of a military unit were natural partners.

By 1913 a symphony orchestra had been added to the bands at Purdue, with many of the musicians playing in both the orchestra and military band.

In 1914 the band expanded to fifty-three members, almost two percent of the student body at that time. By 1916 the band had grown to seventy members, nearly double the number when Emrick had entered Purdue as a freshman a dozen years earlier. He seemed on his way toward his goal of making the band the biggest in the "West."

In 1917 the whims and tastes of the time had an enormous impact on band music at Purdue. Two new bands were added that year, and both had about twenty instrumentalists. They were the men's and women's ukulele orchestras.

The idea of playing in a band was appealing to young musicians, especially when the other choice was to drill with a military unit. There were probably many young men who

SIGNS
Purdue
Purdue

The Roaring '20s

Clockwise from top:

Band members participated in "Doc Erwin's Celebrated Jug Symphony" in 1923–1924.

Drum major from the end of the 1920s.

Mimicking John Philip Sousa's band, Purdue included the whole family of saxophones in their band.

Facing page:

This formal photograph from 1925–1926 depicts eleven ranks of ten men across, a common block band formation for the day.

Purdue

became involved in the band the way Marcus Gilbert did as a freshman in the fall of 1921.

"Military training was compulsory," Gilbert said in a 1986 interview. "The first time they had us standing in the Armory, it was a morning, and it was very hot. We had our uniforms on, and I looked kind of faint. The drill sergeant looked at me and shouted, 'Hey, get out of line until you cool off.' Standing in line [for the Army] was a taste of what I would have to do for the next two years, and I didn't like it."

That same day he saw a band announcement stating certain musicians were needed and that a membership in the band fulfilled Purdue's military obligation. Gilbert signed up.

Edward Lee, class of 1919, played the saxophone in the military band in 1915 and 1916 and remembered band members wearing pigskin puttees and an Army uniform.

"The band had a great reputation, and it was one of the reasons I went to Purdue," said C. W. Hemmer, class of 1921, in a 1986 interview.

One of his earliest memories was trying out for the band when he arrived at the University in 1917. "I was nervous," he said. "But you know, the music they set before me was 'The Stars and Stripes Forever.' I knew that thing from memory. Spotts didn't spend much time with me that day. He left in his typical way and said, 'I think we can use him.'"

Emrick was the sole voice of authority. Those musicians he wanted to play, played; those he didn't want, didn't. He was strict, typical of college instructors of that time, but the members of the band loved him, even though he could appear to an outsider to be insulting when a musician failed to play up to his demands. The students understood what he was doing. He was demanding their best—as any professor would.

"I thought Spotts Emrick was great," Hemmer said. "He was a real buddy of mine. I loved that man. I used to go to his home at the corner of Northwestern and Stadium [avenues]. He had a great, grand piano in his home, and he used to have me play that. But I never called him Spotts. He was always Professor Emrick to me."

"During band rehearsal, whenever anyone couldn't play something right, I remember him going back and showing him how it should be done," Hemmer said. "I remember him once playing the cymbals. You could almost see smoke coming out of them the way he played. He was a perfectionist, and he could play anything. He was a very serious gentleman, but he could laugh sometimes when you cracked a joke. He was a good director. If there was a musician who wasn't doing it right, he could find him, and he'd change chairs right there in practice."

One thing Emrick would not tolerate was a lack of enthusiasm. He expected every person to play with the same total involvement and flair he himself brought to his music.

In the early 1930s, J. D. Legner found out just what Emrick wanted. The band was rehearsing a Wagner piece in the small practice room in the Armory where the music bounced off the walls and reverberated in one's head. Emrick wanted the timpani drum to stand out boldly, and Legner wasn't performing to the director's standards. Emrick dropped his baton, waved his hands, and the band stopped, cold.

"Legner," he shouted. "Have you ever broken a timpani head?"

"No sir," Legner shouted back.

"Well then, let's see if you can," Emrick replied.

Legner hauled off and hit the head hard, but not hard enough to satisfy Emrick.

"Hell, Legner, hit the damn thing," Emrick shouted. "Really lay into it."

By this time Legner was fired up. He raised the mallet over his head, swung his body into the motion, and hit the

Band officers from 1937–1938 pose with Emrick (center).

Popcorn King Orville Redenbacher played a helicon horn in the Purdue band in the 1920s.

drum so hard it sounded like thunder crashing through the roof of the Armory.

It also broke the mallet, and Legner stood there with half a shaft in his hand. Emrick never missed a beat.

"Now you've got it," he shouted. "Do it like that while we're playing."

They went through a lot of mallets in Emrick's days.

In a 1986 interview, Orville Redenbacher, who joined the band as a freshman at Purdue in 1924 and went on to fame as a popcorn king, also remembered the enormous sound of the band in the practice room.

"The first time I was in that room, Spotts raised his baton and everybody started playing, and I couldn't play, I was so overcome by the sound of that 100-member band," he said. "I'll never forget it."

When the band member list reached the triple digits, they marched ten men across and ten men deep. There were probably no bigger college bands in the country, although some others had reached the marching-hundred status. That was a goal to be met but not often surpassed at most universities for the simple reasons that the more men added, the more complex marching formations became, the more music had to be purchased, and the more expensive it became to travel.

Everyone remembered Emrick's tough practices.

"One day we did something wrong, and he assigned the whole bunch of us to do double time around the field," Hemmer said. "Spotts was a perfectionist, and the band loved him for it. He was a big fellow, and he wore that uniform well. He had a good loud voice. You could hear him all over. When it was time to practice, we were all ready to go. There was no messing around. When he came into the room and took his position, it was time to perform. We were very proud."

While he was strict, Emrick was also known for one particular prank.

At the first practice in the fall after the start of school, he would sit at the back of band in the Armory as it played the Army "Caisson Song" with the familiar words: "Over hill, over dale, as we hit the dusty trail, and those caissons go rolling along. Counter march, right about, hear the wagon soldiers shout, while the caissons go rolling along . . . ."

When the band reached the lyrics "then it's hi, hi, yee for the field artillery," Emrick would pull out a .38-caliber snub-nosed revolver loaded with blanks and fire it into the air three times.

Inside the Armory the gunshots sounded like cannon fire, and unsuspecting freshmen would fall off of their chairs. Sitting at the back of the band, Emrick, too, would almost fall off his chair—laughing.

John Bernard Moorehouse, who graduated in 1921 and played the bass in the band for three years, remembered Emrick as being one of the innovators of the day.

"He must have had a perfect ear for pitch," Moorehouse said. "If someone was faltering, he'd take their instrument and play it correctly. You learned the first time you went to rehearsal, when he reached out with his baton and tapped his music rack, that it was a sign for perfect silence. If you blared a couple notes after that, you never did it again. He would embarrass you in front of the whole crowd. He was perfectly fair, but the only way he could direct the band was to have absolute control, which he maintained. He didn't embarrass you unless you had it coming."

At one practice a bassoonist had a solo part, and Emrick stopped the band right in the middle of rehearsing the piece.

"My God, what's the matter with the tone of that instrument?" he shouted.

"It sounds all right to me," said the musician.

"It sounds like a shingle flapping on a roof during a windstorm," Emrick replied.

Early version of the Block "P" with musicians marching in opposite directions.

The 1930s

Clockwise from top:

Twelve band members play glockenspiels, featured instruments in the band during the 1939–1940 school year.

Herald trumpets in Block "P" formation in the 1940s.

Emrick directed the band at the Hall of Science Building, Chicago World's Fair "A Century of Progress," in 1935.

Facing page:

Band prepares to board buses before the road opening at George Ade's on October 4, 1932.

INDIANAPOLIS - DANVILLE - CHAMPAIGN
PEORIA - BLOOMINGTON, ILL. - SPRINGFIELD, ILL.
COLUMBUS - DAYTON - LOUISVILLE, KY.
SPECIAL
BOB BROWN

By 1937 the band's headquarters were located in the basement of the Armory.

By the early 1920s, Emrick and the Purdue band already had set records: in 1907 it became the first band to break formation and form a block letter; in 1919 it became the first band to carry all the colors of the schools in the Big Ten; in 1920 it became the first band to play the opponent school's fight song.

The year 1921 marked the entrance of the "World's Largest Drum," which became one of the most lasting symbols of the band and Purdue University (read more on the drum in chapter six).

On several occasions during the mid- to late 1920s, John Philip Sousa and his famed military band came to Purdue and performed.

During his Purdue visits, Sousa performed with his own group in concert. Then Emrick led Sousa's band in "The Stars and Stripes Forever," and Sousa led the Purdue band. The two bands also played as one.

During the Indiana State Fair in September 1928, a Purdue band concert was carried by WLS radio, which was out of Chicago. On December 18, 1928, people in Lafayette and throughout a large part of the Midwest were able to stay in their homes and listen to WLS as the band performed another live radio performance from its concert hall on campus.

By 1928 the band was using moving pictures—home movies that Emrick would later shoot himself—to view and study and practice formations. As early as 1930, Emrick also used recordings of rehearsals to find the weak spots he might have missed.

The climax of the 1928 season came fittingly at the Purdue versus Indiana game when, according to the Purdue Alumni Association magazine, the *Alumnus*, the band "successfully displayed the most complicated group of formations ever attempted by a college band." The band played continuously forming, "IU," "PU," the words "Indiana" and "Purdue," and finally a gigantic "P."

As they made the formations, the band members played several Big Ten school songs and added yells to their routine. The spelling of the words "Indiana" and "Purdue" was modeled after electric signs with the letters moving across. The letters emerged from the mass formation of the band, moved across the field, and dissolved again into a mass formation.

The marching style of the band was attracting so much attention that in the fall of 1929, a Fox Movietone News crew filmed the band for its newsreels. In 1933 the Purdue band was featured during two days of concerts at the Chicago World's Fair, "A Century of Progress."

There were many other eventful trips for the band, such as the 1933 journey to South Bend. The Purdue football team beat Notre Dame 19-0, and at the end of the game Irish fans took the field, started making snowballs, and rushed to where the Purdue band was sitting.

Emrick was able to stop the assault by having the band members play the Notre Dame fight song and every Irish melody with which the group was familiar.

The Purdue band was winning distinctions, but it wasn't "the biggest in the West" as Emrick had envisioned. At least, it couldn't claim that title in 1934.

According to the *Detroit News* and other historical sources, the Illinois band had 175 members; the Wisconsin band had 160; the Ohio State band had 120; Indiana had 110; and Purdue and Michigan had 100. The University of Chicago band was the smallest in the Big Ten with 85 musicians.

The lighted band show at Northwestern's Dyche Stadium in the fall of 1935 had its origins in the spring of that year when the band marched in Louisville at the Kentucky Derby Festival Parade on April 29, 1935.

Emrick's Formations

Besides the Block "P," Emrick went on to other, even more complicated formations that were befitting a military band.

To learn formations, Emrick and the Operations ("Ops") crew would review the hand-drawn diagram and pound stakes into the grass field at appropriate places so that band members would know where to stand for the formation.

The modern drill field, which is asphalt, has various markings, and students utilize computer-generated drill charts to learn where to stand.

Letters that spell words like "Purdue" must be three times as tall as they are wide to be easily readable from the fans' perspective in the stands.

Clockwise from top: Band members spell out "Purdue" in the 1950 football season; Field formation from the 1939–1940 season; Formation of "PU" from the 1950 football game versus Miami.

BEAT THAT DRUM!

Alan Reynolds, Class of 1943, has this memory of Emrick:

"From 1940 to 1943, I played baritone under Spotts Emrich's direction. He is one of the most unforgettable men I have ever known. He made sure the drummers always had extra sticks and his instructions were 'If the head breaks, just beat the hell out of the rims. And congratulations for doing it.' In marching band practice you made sure you lifted your feet at least six inches or you would get a guide-on pole in your butt.

At concert band practice in the Music Hall the student conductor would call off the piece and the place in the music – and then we might wait five minutes, or five seconds, for Spotts to run in, grabbing his baton on the way and start the moment he hit the podium. Woe unto anyone who did not hit that first note. He directed sitting in that old swivel chair, usually with eyes closed but ears full open."

Since the parade was at night, it was decided to add electric lights to the larger band instruments, to the drum major's baton, to the top of the flagpoles, and to the glockenspiels. The Purdue "World's Largest Drum" was lighted, as were the sousaphones. The night of the parade, the lighted band marched the several miles and received a loud ovation from the crowd.

In a letter to the Fulton County Historical Society in 1983, band member Byron Legg wrote, "For five miles, before nearly half a million people we were cheered almost every step of the way. The train got back into Lafayette at 3 a.m., and by the time we were home it was broad daylight, but I was so high I could not have slept under any circumstances."

After the great success with the lighted band in Louisville, the performance was repeated in Lafayette during a ceremonial parade, and Emrick had no intention of dropping the idea. He wanted to keep it going, and the opportunity arose the following fall at the football game against Northwestern.

When Emrick heard about the night scheduling of the game, he dusted off the light show plans from the prior spring, and he added some innovations.

The halftime show that night in Dyche Stadium began in total darkness. All the band members' caps were lighted at a single moment when they marched out of the end zone playing "Anchors Aweigh." As the band moved down the field, tiny anchors fell away until the band was composed of seven anchors.

The big bass drum was missing through all of this, and there were no colored lights, which had been featured in the past.

But the band wasn't through. It marched from the center of the field toward the end zone, turned to march back, and suddenly the "World's Largest Drum" was in view, fully lighted in the middle of the marchers. Then, just as suddenly, a shot was fired, and colored lights on instruments throughout the band were turned on.

"The rows of lights moved in alternate directions giving the appearance of an electric sign in which the lights seem to move," E. F. Kueck, class of 1936, wrote in the *Purdue Alumnus*. "A second drum major stepped from behind the drum, which was now revolving in the center of the 'P' [formation] and [he] rapidly twirled a baton with a kerosene flame on each end. He seemed to be circled by a ring of fire as he twisted it behind his back and under his legs. From the beginning to the end of the performance, the crowd stood on its feet and cheered every move of the band."

The band repeated its lighted marching show at the Kentucky Derby Festival Parade in 1936.

With his great electrical feat accomplished, during the 1937–1938 year Emrick resigned from his position as professor of electrical engineering and devoted his full energies to the band.

In 1939 the cornerstone was laid at what would later be named the Edward C. Elliott Hall of Music, marking the beginning of the final phase of construction on the landmark that would house Purdue's musical groups, both vocal and instrumental.

There were about 150 members in the band in 1939, the largest yet. Plans were already underway to enlarge it to 300, so it might have been no coincidence that the new band practice room in the Hall of Music was built to seat 300.

The Hall of Music was one of Emrick's great dreams. He spent many long hours planning and working on the band shell at the back of the great hall.

"A great deal of his own time, thoughts and imagination went into the design of the shell, and he finally had an appropriate home for his great band that for years had been

Clockwise from top left: Formal portrait of Purdue Symphony Band from the 1935–1936 season. Prior to building of Elliott Hall, many concerts were held at Jefferson High School; Instrument storage and rehearsal space in the 1930s in the Armory; Pontiac Hour broadcast on NBC from Memorial Gym, 1937–1938.

quartered in the basement of the Armory," Dr. M. Hunter Smith, a drum major in the late 1930s, wrote in his memories of Purdue.

With the onset of World War II, Emrick placed the band at the disposal of bond sale rallies and any other patriotic events that could possibly be worked into the students' schedules. In 1942 the Purdue band joined movie star and Indiana native Carole Lombard in a big bond-sale rally in Indianapolis, one of the largest in the country to date. It was a great success, and Lombard told the people of her home state that she knew they could be relied upon. She died in an airline accident as she was returning to California after the drive was successfully completed.

"Big" was still the operative word with the Purdue band once the war ended. Its membership soon surpassed 180, nowhere near the 300 hoped for at the onset of the war, but much better than the war years when band membership dropped below 100.

The "World's Largest Drum" was not being featured at this time because of a broken head, but the band might have had the world's largest glockenspiel section—twenty-four of them in all. Musicians carried these U-shaped instruments on short poles, striking the bars with small mallets.

In the post-World War II years, many band members were returning servicemen in their late twenties, and Emrick treated them differently than younger college students. He gave the combat veterans and active military the respect they deserved.

Morgan Henika received a Purdue bachelor's degree in Metallurgical Engineering 1948 and wrote to the University about his memories.

"I came to Purdue in June 1944 as a freshman/Apprentice Seaman in the V-12 program," he said. "I had played sousaphone in my Lakewood, Ohio high school band. Spotts interviewed me, had me play a few bars and told me to report for band practice. We practiced behind the fieldhouse. Spotts' ever-present Chow dog occasionally would get in the way and Spotts, on his long, spindly legs, would chase the dog firing his blank pistol and cursing at him. Spotts wasn't appreciative of the band's laughter at this antic!"

In 1951 the marching band came out with its first album, a 10-inch, 78-RPM disc appropriately titled "Hail Purdue."

The Purdue band in 1954 was a military marching band, just as it had been in 1905. However, times were changing and marching bands were changing. In 1954 Purdue changed. It was Emrick's last year as director. After forty-nine

In the 1940s, fans, cheerleaders, and band members traveled on the same train, such as this one in 1946.

Facing page: One of the first formal practices of the Symphony Band in Room 15 in Elliott Hall when it opened in 1941. Today, the band still rehearses in this room.

The War Years

Clockwise from top:

Purdue band at Navy Day Parade in May 1942.

Halftime salute to WWII veterans in the late 1940s.

Performing at patriotic events has always been important to the band, exhibited by this performance in 1953–1954.

Band members stop for dinner at northwest Indiana's famous Teibel's restaurant after performing at a football game versus Northwestern in 1945.

years as the head of the band, he retired. He had reached the mandatory retirement age of seventy.

On Sunday, May 9, 1954, Emrick directed a special Purdue band in a final concert during Mother's Day weekend. The concert band, composed of eighty-five handpicked men, played in the Hall of Music. At the end of the performance, Emrick turned and faced the audience. He bluntly announced that he was not leaving voluntarily but was being forced to leave due to the University's mandatory retirement age.

Emrick returned to his hometown, Rochester, and lived in his family's cottage on Lake Manitou. Every year he was invited back to direct the band for a special guest appearance, and sometimes he accepted.

In his band memories, Smith wrote, "I think that Spotts was a very private person, except when he was rehearsing his band. Then he had a temper like an elephant with an impacted molar. He spent hours listening to recordings of classics played by the greatest orchestras under the best conductors in order to know how to direct them when the symphonic band played them. He would buy the best instruments in the world if he had a solo-quality musician in the band."

"Spotts would work at the band headquarters to all hours of the night, and much to my dismay, he expected the band officers to do the same," Edward Barnes, who played in the 1940s, wrote about his years with Emrick. "He was a demanding, caustic S.O.B., and I loved him for it. He made my job as drum major easier. After serving in the Marine Corps for three years [and being away from campus], I walked into his office, and he said, 'Oh, you again. If you want your job back, you got it.' He didn't say, 'Nice to see you.' [He] just went back to his charts. The only time he and I tangled was in the fall of 1946 when we were preparing for a performance at Ohio State. He wanted me to prance around like the drum major at Ohio State. I refused and told him we were an ROTC unit and I had more class than that. He guffawed through his famous megaphone and replied, 'Damn it, you're right.'"

Emrick liked to give character-building lectures, and he fired up the band with enthusiastic speeches before performances.

Emrick is presented with a plaque recognizing the creation of the Block "P," the first formation in college band history, in 1957.

Games Slayter—the inventor of Fiberglass, the benefactor of Slayter Center on the Purdue campus, and a Purdue band member—once called Emrick the greatest influence in his life.

Such was the complexity of the man who was the heart and soul and spirit of the Purdue band program for nearly a half century.

He had taught more than six thousand students.

He died on July 28, 1965, in Rochester at the age of eighty-one from a cerebral hemorrhage.

A memorial resolution on the life of Emrick was prepared by several Purdue staff members and read into the 1966-1967 minutes of the Purdue Senate. It said in part: "He considered the purpose of the band to be not only for music but for character building."

Four years after Emrick's death, one of the "band boys" became the first man on the moon.

Neil Armstrong arrived on the Purdue campus in the fall of 1947 and joined the "All-American" Marching Band as an ROTC option. He played the baritone horn and a little bass and had experience playing in his high school marching band.

Asked how many instruments he currently plays, Armstrong answered, "None. But in my youth I played seven."

"I enjoyed the music and the band [at Purdue] and some interesting trips to away football games, the Indianapolis 500, etc.," Armstrong commented.

He also performed in the Symphonic Band at Purdue.

Emrick, Armstrong said, "was a curmudgeon and easily the most colorful of all my professors at Purdue. He was an icon, being the first director to have his band break formation and make something other than a rectangular outline. This was the highest quality musical organization with which I had ever been associated. I felt honored to be part of the best band in the Big Ten."

Right: Neil Armstrong accepts gifts from Kappa Kappa Psi members at a Purdue Symphonic Band concert following his return from the moon. Armstrong took this Kappa Kappa Psi pin (above) with him on his historic 1969 trip.

CHAPTER THREE

TRADITION GOES GLOBAL

The Al G. Wright Years

By 1954 there had been seven Purdue University presidents but only one director of bands, and he was reluctantly heading into mandatory retirement at the age of seventy.

Through the first half of the twentieth century, Paul Spotts Emrick *was* Purdue bands. He had absolute authority in the band department, running it his way. His style was one that gave the band a place in history; he had set the pace for other bands to follow.

But times had changed considerably from 1905 when Emrick began directing the band. The military marching he still favored had given way to a popular, free-flowing style. The marching pace had changed. The style of music had changed. The band formations had changed.

It was time for Purdue bands to change, and with the retirement of Emrick, President Frederick L. Hovde and the Purdue University Board of Trustees looked for someone who would carry the band tradition into a new era.

In Al G. Wright, Purdue found a man who, at the age of thirty-eight, was a little more than half Emrick's age and who would fashion himself into a legend quickly.

Like Emrick, Wright would lead the Purdue band department and the marching band until his retirement. Like Emrick, he would start traditions at Purdue that would be copied nationwide. Like Emrick, he demanded the best from his students and made them give more than they often knew they had within them.

But unlike Emrick, Wright did not come from a military band background. He was a showman, a performer.

His idea of a band was one that moved quickly all around the football field, playing to everyone—those sitting on the fifty-yard line on both sides of the stadium and the people with seats in the end zones. His band formed letters and designs and drew pictures for the halftime crowds at Ross-Ade and football stadiums across the nation.

During his performances he wanted something happening on the field in front of everyone throughout the entire halftime show, and that required lots of people—lots of musicians, lots of baton twirlers, lots of flag carriers. He was not satisfied with just carrying the flag of each Big Ten university. Wright added four lines of ten flags each—forty flags—four from each Big Ten school. The Big Ten flags totally disappeared in the 1980s and 1990s, but the tradition was returned by Director of Bands Jay Gephart in 2006.

Within months of his arrival at Purdue, Wright added more majorettes to the band—and with short skirts. He brought back the big drum (read more about the drum in chapter six), added spats, and eventually changed the band uniform. He increased the number of drum majors from one to two.

He introduced featured solo twirlers—the Golden Girl, the Girl in Black, the Silver Twins (read more about the Silver Twins in chapter five)—and the "I Am an American" flag presentation (read more about this presentation in chapter ten). He and his select band members performed everywhere from hot, dusty bullrings in South America to Radio City Music Hall with the Rockettes in New York City.

For the next twenty-seven years, band members would give him nicknames like "Tyrant of the Tower," and they would look back on those days as some of the most rewarding, meaningful, and fun of their lives.

Wright was perfect for the role of director of bands at Purdue when he arrived in the mid-1950s. He was young and handsome with crew cut hair and a beautiful wife, Gladys, who was also a very talented musician and band director. He was filled with ideas and energy, and he wanted to integrate the band even deeper into the culture of the University.

Previous page: Al Wright works with student musicians.

Record from Al Wright era featuring 126-member Symphonic Band.

Left: Alumni band from the mid-1950s.

Right: Ever since the creation of the "World's Largest Drum," big instruments have been popular features with the band including this large gong.

Yet when Wright was first asked to interview for the job, he was not even certain where Purdue was located.

He was born in London, England, in 1916 to British parents who struggled during and after World War I. His father was a tool and dye worker, and in 1923 they immigrated to the United States and settled in Pontiac, Michigan, where Wright's father found a job with General Motors.

The young Wright had a talent for music, especially the French horn. It was a talent his band director spotted in junior high school. Wright eventually found himself performing with one of the best high school bands in the country. When he graduated from high school in 1933, in the midst of the Great Depression, he was offered a band scholarship at the University of Miami in Florida.

The University of Miami was founded in 1925, and Wright said it was trying to establish itself in the 1930s. "They decided if they were going to be a good university they needed to have a basketball team, a football team, a band, and a symphony orchestra," Wright said in an interview about his life stored at the Purdue Libraries Archives. "My high school band director had contact with them and they were looking for a French horn player. They were offering full scholarships—room, board, tuition, everything—for people who would play in their band and orchestra as well as for football and basketball players. I think they took about thirty of us from the Detroit area."

Wright graduated from the University of Miami in 1937, and soon he began teaching at Miami High School. The school included students from throughout Dade County, and he quickly attracted some of the best young musicians in the southern tip of Florida. He also became a codirector of the city's Orange Bowl Festival and received his master's degree from the University of Miami in 1947. His high school band was so well respected that it gained a national reputation. He was going someplace, but he didn't know where.

In 1948 Wright was offered the assistant band director position at the University of Illinois. He turned it down. He wanted to run his own program. He had his own ideas; he had his own style; and he didn't want to conform what he was doing to the concepts of someone else.

Band composer Harold L. Walters is the person credited with bringing Wright to Purdue. Walters is recognized as one

Drum majors step out to lead the band onto the field.

A coed protects herself from the "deafening roar" of the "World's Largest Drum" in a 1957 publicity photograph.

of the most prolific U.S. band composers. He was chief arranger for the U.S. Navy Band in Washington D.C. and head composer for Rubank Publishers in Chicago and then Miami until his death in 1984. Walters was familiar with Wright's work with the high school band in Florida. He had been a judge at competitions Wright's band entered.

When Emrick retired, Purdue University received a stack of applications for the position. One afternoon, in the spring of 1954, Purdue Trustee J. Ralph Thompson met with Walters. Both men lived in Seymour, Indiana.

Purdue had never recruited a band director, and without the College of Music faculty to advise the board members, they needed direction. No one on the search committee was really knowledgeable about bands.

"Harold," Thompson said, "we're hiring a new band director, and we've got a stack of applications two feet high. What are we going to do?"

"I'll tell you what you're going to do," Walters said. "You're going to throw them all away and call a young man named Al Wright in Florida."

By coincidence, one of Wright's former high school band students, May Jewel Gong, was a respected symphony band clarinetist at Purdue, and she had gone so far as to lobby President Hovde to give the job to Wright. But Wright hadn't applied for the position, so the University wrote him a letter and asked him to come for a visit.

"Harold called me," Wright says. "He said you're going to be in Chicago for a band meeting. I'll be there, too, and I'll drive you down to Purdue."

Walters delivered Wright and Gladys to the office of Vice President and Executive Dean Frank Hockema. After some time with Hockema, they all went to dinner with President Hovde, Vice President and Treasurer R. B. Stewart, and Athletic Director Red Mackey.

"I was scared," Wright says. "We all sat around a table. I picked my words carefully. "

Hovde was quiet throughout the dinner, but he finally spoke. "Well, young man, if we bring you to Purdue, what's your plan?" he asked.

Wright held up two fingers. "One, I'll have a good band here," he said. "And two, it'll cost you a lot of money."

Wright smiled. Hovde, who was fiscally cautious, saw the joke and laughed. The offer did not come immediately, but it came in time, through the mail. There were some delays in sealing the deal when one of Wright's letters to Purdue ended up in Lafayette, Louisiana.

Although Purdue had no music school, and although only weeks before Wright needed to ask his high school principal

One of the first Band Days in 1954, where Indiana high school bands came to perform with the Purdue "All-American" Marching Band.

Top: Having fun at the December Band Awards Banquet in 1959. The tradition of band banquets started in 1957.

Bottom: Tuba "bull" plays the game with a Purdue drum major turned matador for a 1950s halftime show.

where Purdue was located, and although it meant a move from the mild South to outdoor performances in the cold Midwest winter, Wright accepted the offer.

"For me it was a marvelous opportunity to be invited to come from a high school and be Director of Bands at a Big Ten university," he said.

He was offered $7,200 a year—the same pay that Emrick had received. Wright only made $4,000 at Miami, so the Purdue offer was a big financial boost for the young couple who had only married nine months before.

The University's interest in Wright was best summed up by R. B. Stewart.

"I was intrigued with him," Stewart said in an interview conducted in the mid-1980s. Stewart, who is considered a major figure in developing Purdue, died in 1988. "Al was a showman. He knew how to use the band for the betterment of the university. The only way you could get anywhere was to use the band as a showpiece. He could do it. And he did do it. Al put life in the band program. He made it into real theater, a show, an attractive thing."

Wright first went to work at Purdue in the summer of 1954, arriving with his crew cut and a bow tie. "My God," he would say years later looking at his picture in a scrapbook, "it looks like he just graduated from high school." He received his instructions from Hovde.

"Young man, I want you to make some changes," the president said. But a vice president added, "Be careful. You're going to step on some toes; be careful of those who have corns."

Wright moved slowly, at least as slowly as he could, considering his excitement and deep interest in getting the show on the road.

He spent the summer studying what Emrick had been doing and decided to keep everything and just take it a little further. He kept the Army uniforms, but he added white spats so the band members' feet would stand out when they marched. He put plumes in their hats and increased the size of the flag corps.

During the first year, some alumni groused about his changes, but Mackey came to his defense. "Every time we get a new coach, you're the same people who grumble about him doing new things," Mackey said. "Leave this band director alone."

After about two years, people began to see what Wright and the band were trying to accomplish, and progress accelerated.

"When I came here they had these traditions, and you just don't go in and wipe the slate clean," Wright said. "I accepted everything they had. Except, I sent out a solo female twirler in a short skirt."

To say that this act rocked the Purdue tradition of a male military band is an understatement (read more about this tradition in chapter five).

Wright looked for ways to involve the band in Purdue events. One of the first things he did was take the Purdue Symphonic Band to R. B. Stewart's home for a pig roast.

"R. B. Stewart brought people in from all over the country, and he had a big cookout," Wright said. "I had Harold Walters write us a 'Fanfare For a Roasted Pig.' We played it when they brought the pig out and the band played backup music during dinner. It got Stewart interested in us because we weren't afraid to do a little bit extra. Then he heard us at commencement. We pretty much revised the band's participation in commencement. They had all that dead time when they passed out diplomas, and instead of just sitting there, we played almost continuously."

Wright Gets Music's Best

Some of the era's biggest names in the music business came to play with the Purdue Bands.

Clockwise from top left:

Arthur Fiedler consults with Symphonic Band members as guest conductor, 1959–1960.

Golden Girl Valerie Brown with Mitch Miller, 1968.

"Tonight Show" trumpeter Doc Severinsen performs at halftime in Ross-Ade Stadium, 1970.

Al and Gladys Wright with noted trumpet player Rafael Mendez, 1955.

Dizzy Gillespie autographs a poster before a 1962 concert.

Former President Dwight D. Eisenhower reviews the band at the Purdue Airport during the 1962–1963 season.

At Wright's first Purdue commencement, he and Walters had worked out the arrangement of "Pomp and Circumstance" so the band would raise the key just as Hovde started up the steps to the stage.

Hovde noticed. He turned toward Wright and touched his red cap in a formal greeting. Then he smiled and held up two fingers, remember the two points the band director had made during the interview.

"He always gave me whatever I asked for," Wright says. "But I was careful not to ask for too much."

Still, not everyone was happy. Wright was summoned to the athletic offices by Mackey one day. The telephone call had been terse. When he arrived at Mackey's office, he found another man seated in a chair, looking somber. This was one person Mackey had apparently not been able to win over to Wright's side.

"We've got a problem here," Mackey said. "This man is not happy with you. His concession sales at the stadium are down because everyone is staying in the stands at halftime to watch the band." Then Mackey broke out in laughter.

Emrick had taken the Purdue Symphonic Band to play around the state, often at high schools. Wright based his performances with this band at Elliott Hall of Music and invited guest conductors of national fame to come in and take the podium.

These conductors were often well known to the general public—people such as Arthur Fiedler from the Boston Pops Orchestra took up the baton at the Hall of Music. Other guest conductors included Leroy Anderson, Skitch Henderson, Edwin Franko Goldman, Mitch Miller, and Sir Vivian Dunn.

In the spring of 1955, Wright invited Paul Lavalle to conduct the Purdue Symphonic Band. Lavalle was director of a national NBC radio show called "Band of America," sponsored by Cities Service Oil Company. He and Wright had been friends for years.

What Wright did not know was that the president of Cities Service was a Purdue graduate. When the company president learned that Lavalle would guest conduct in West Lafayette, he sent the entire radio show to Indiana, and Purdue became the national "Band of the Week."

Lavalle arrived on campus right after an early spring snowstorm. Wright never missed an opportunity for publicity. He had band majorette Toby Huth, of Lexington, Kentucky, on hand at the airport to present his guest conductor with cross-country skis to use in getting around campus. He also saw to it that a newspaper photographer was on hand to record the event.

They gave away tickets to the show, and Elliott Hall of Music was filled to capacity.

The radio program aired at 8 p.m. on Monday, March 28, 1955, less than a year after Wright had been named director of bands at Purdue. "This was probably the one single event that had the most influence in making the Purdue band program known nationally," Wright said.

It was a night of popular and patriotic music with Dr. Roy Shield conducting the Cities Service band in New York City

The Band at Radio City Music Hall

Purdue musicians performed at Radio City Music Hall for four summers in the 1960s–1970s. In the 1963 show, Purdue musicians dressed as servicemen to fit the theme of the show. *Clockwise from top:* Six Purdue band members don't mind being crowded into a convertible with a Rockette for a backstage picture; Purdue band members tour New York City during free time; Climax of 1963 show was an emotional re-creation of the flag raising at Iwo Jima.

Golden Girl June Ciampa practices tricks with band.

and Lavalle and Wright conducting the Purdue band in West Lafayette. Everything from "The Light Cavalry Overture" to "God of Our Fathers" to the "Dwight D. Eisenhower March" to "Hail Purdue" slipped into the program.

The band had played on regional radio before, including the popular WLS out of Chicago, but this was the biggest audience for the band to date—a national audience. It brought recognition to Wright, it brought recognition to the band, and it brought recognition to Purdue.

It also brought gratitude from Hovde, who was interviewed on the NBC radio show. This gave him the opportunity to talk about his university to alumni and prospective students all over the country.

"The show helped me out a lot," Wright said. "All of a sudden I was getting the kind of attention that the Glee Club had been getting. And people were ready for it. All over the country kids heard the Purdue band and started to come here. I didn't need a school of music. They would come anyway. And let's face it, engineers are pretty bright kids, and so are the kids studying sciences. Not only did I have pretty good players, I had smart kids and young people who were disciplined."

Wright did end one tradition: Emrick's harsh audition style.

"Spotts auditioned [students] for the band," Wright said. "It was tough and everybody said they would come out shaking. He was pretty rough on kids and you were supposed to be rough on kids in those days. But they just hated those auditions. So what I said is, 'Join the band, then we'll listen to you play and we'll find a place for you.'"

Wright worked hard and expected band members to do the same.

Henri Evans, class of 1964 and a self-described "terrible trumpet player," said Wright was destined early in life to be successful at whatever he did. Evans had known Wright for years during high school summer band camp before enrolling at Purdue. He got to know the director even better while a band member at Purdue and in later years as an alumnus.

"Al would have been a great football coach, a great politician, and an outstanding businessman," Evans said. "He would have been good at whatever he chose to do because he had high standards and he never compromised. Never. He was the single toughest guy I ever was around. He was fair, but he was totally unyielding. He made the band program what it is today, and his effect will be felt for many years to come. My band experience was probably the most worthwhile experience I had in college."

Tom Tesmer, class of 1970 and a trombone player in the band, laughed warmly talking about Wright. "He was a son of a gun," Tesmer said.

Tom Lester, also from the class of 1970, agreed. Lester said: "He had very definite ideas about what he wanted to get out of us. He made us very much aware that if we screwed up, we were wasting the time of four hundred people."

June Ciampa, the fifth Golden Girl, said. "He was tough, tough, tough. When I was a freshman and came here, people said, 'Wait until you see him. He'll make you shiver.' He made us all grow up. He taught us a lot about the real world. If I had threads hanging from my costume, he'd say, 'Hey, that's a personal problem. You can take care of it.' You knew where you stood with him. It didn't matter if it was raining or snowing and freezing outside, he made you want to give 100 percent, and I really believe the band always gave 100 percent."

Jon Thuerbach, a drum major who graduated in 1979, said. "Wright was really tough, but he knew how to put a super show together. I respected him for his toughness. Everyone knew how it was going to be, and everyone accepted it and worked hard, and we had a fantastic band."

Wright Era Formations

Below: Birds-eye view of the "Floating Purdue" formation. Wright used photos like this, and film, to make sure everything was done "Wright." He also employed toy soldiers to move about a model field when he was dreaming up the formations.

Top left: Marking Purdue's Centennial Celebration in 1969.

Bottom left, Wright brings his show band style to Memorial Stadium at Indiana University.

Wright's Formations: Floating Purdue & Locomotive

Ever since Emrick's era, the band had spelled out "Purdue" on the football field. Al Wright decided to make it an active formation that would move down the field, so he created the "Floating Purdue" that is still used today, here at the Champs Bowl in 2007.

Facing page: When Wright came to Purdue, he wanted to have more images on the field, and he created the "Locomotive," seen here in its earliest version in 1955 (inset), and a current view captured at a 2007 night game against Ohio State.

PURDUE
PURDUE

A drum major struts down field beside the band, 1960.

The band under Wright would not only perform outdoors no matter what the weather, it would also practice outside in the heat or in a blizzard.

One late fall afternoon, on one of those Indiana days when winter seems to come right at the end of summer with wet, near-freezing temperatures, Jack Mollenkopf, the coach of Purdue football, had his team outside practicing.

The players grumbled about the miserable weather and asked the coach if they could finish the workout inside in the gym. However, Mollenkopf could see and hear the band working through its routine for the coming Saturday afternoon.

"No one on this football team is going inside as long as the band is still out here playing," Mollenkopf told the players in no uncertain terms.

The team finished the practice outside.

"Wright had total control; the band was never out of control because of the way he ran it," said Gary Cummings. He graduated in the late 1970s and was winner of an Outstanding Marching Bandsman Award. "In my freshman year when I came to Purdue I was accustomed to getting places on time. I went to the freshman meeting, and as I was walking through the doors, they were locking the doors behind me. People kept coming, but Wright made them stand behind the locked doors for fifteen or twenty minutes. When the doors were opened, he told them, 'That's the last time you'll ever be late while you're in the band.'"

He had a strict rule on trips. He couldn't watch three hundred or more students. He told band members that if they were not on the buses when the buses were ready to leave, the buses would leave without them. More than one Golden Girl had to find alternate means of transportation when she was late for a departure. The rule stood for everyone.

One year, on a return trip home, Wright was late. The buses left without him.

If both the band and the football team spent a lot of time out in the miserable weather practicing and performing, members of both organizations also spent a lot of time in the film rooms after a Saturday afternoon game. Wright filmed all the performances, and by Monday afternoon he had the film developed, reviewed, and would go over everything in detail. He had a flashlight pointer he would use to highlight mistakes.

"If you made the slightest error, we pointed to it," Wright said. "The fact was, if you were three inches out of line that was wrong. By doing this it got to the point where some of our formations were flawless."

The fact that they worked as hard as athletes, and often harder, was never lost on the members of the band. It's no coincidence they call themselves "jocks"—"band jocks."

"I probably spent as much time in the band program as the athletes did in their programs," Evans says. "People called us 'band jocks.' We were always at the Hall of Music. We were there at 3 in the afternoon, and we wouldn't check out until 6 or 7 at night. We went to all the home football and basketball games and some of the away games. I had that trumpet glued to my mouth for four years, and I loved every minute of it."

The work, the time, the tension, and the rewards for a job well done—the band has always meant something special for the performers. It is more than just music and marching.

"One of the biggest problems you have in coming to a major university is getting lost in the shuffle," Lester said. "Being with the band provided a home for me."

It was home, but it was a man's home. The "All-American" Marching Band was composed of all male musicians. Women only performed with it as majorettes, although it was required that they also be able to play instruments (read more about this topic in chapter five).

Women were not barred from playing instruments in the band. It was just a matter of none applying, Wright said. It would be several more years before women would try out for instrumental positions in the band, and when they did, they were accepted. The band also continued as an arm of the Reserve Officers Training Corps.

Into the mid-1960s, all male students at Purdue still had to take two years of ROTC, and that requirement could be fulfilled by playing in the band. In fact, when that requirement was finally dropped in the fall of 1965 during the Vietnam War era, Wright and others were concerned that membership in the band might drop as a result. Instead, membership went up.

"I came here at a time when bands were getting big," Wright said. "The Purdue band was always one of the larger bands in the Big Ten. And I kept adding to it. As fast as they came in, I kept making the drills bigger and bigger and bigger. We were always about the largest marching band in the country. As far as the audience is concerned, if you march the greatest and play the loudest and you're the biggest band, then you're the best."

In all its years of performing, the Purdue "All-American" Marching Band can boast a perfect record. It has never lost a halftime show. But no matter how large the Purdue band was, Wright made it look minuscule compared to another group he conducted at Ross-Ade Stadium.

He wanted to boost attendance at Ross-Ade on fall Saturday afternoons, and he knew how to accomplish this goal. He invited high school bands from all over the state to come and perform.

HEY YOU NO. 72

Students of his era often quote Wright as telling them, "Perfect practices make perfect performances." However, he says, that is their slant on what he really told them.

"What I said was every rehearsal is a performance," he said. "When you're in a rehearsal, you sit right, you play right, and you play as though someone was listening. We were very direct with the students. In outdoor marching band rehearsal everyone wore a number. We never addressed anyone by name. I'd say, '72, get where you belong.' I remember at the end of one season Number 72 was famous. He was a goof-off. No one knew his name, but when you said '72' everybody knew who you were talking about. By using numbers instead of names it gave a little anonymity to things."

Practice time on a grassy field on Third Street.

In the 1950s he would invite as many as one hundred Indiana high school bands. Eighty would show up, and he would have as many as eight thousand prep students out on the field performing. They not only helped to fill the stadium, but their parents bought tickets. The program helped to inspire young musicians to consider coming to Purdue where they could major in their chosen careers and have fun in the band.

In later years when there wasn't room to fit all the bands in the stadium seats, Wright would invite just the best high school bands in the state to perform for a game.

In addition to conducting the marching band, Wright also conducted the Purdue Symphonic Band and had other responsibilities. He was also expected to lead a pep band that performed at basketball games. That, Wright said, was asking too much.

"I never conducted a basketball band," he said. "In thirty years I went to three basketball games. I told them I wouldn't conduct the basketball band. I had too many other things to do. I needed an assistant."

In 1955 he got one, Robert McEmber, who came from the faculty of what was then Western Michigan College. McEmber took over the basketball band and a variety band and assisted with the marching band. Wright continued adding staff to the department. Roger Heath and Larry Mallett were two assistants who stayed a number of years.

During the late 1950s, the band also began to make use of advertising, not only to promote itself, but to replace instruments and purchase new ones. The ads appeared in a number of national musical publications, and they didn't cost the University a dime. Instrument and band equipment companies paid the bill.

"We used certain brands of instruments, but we never really did endorse them," Wright said. "The only thing the companies could say was that the Purdue band used their product. And we only appeared in advertisements for things we used and purchased."

But the band got a deal on the purchase. One day a salesman delivered thirty-two clarinets worth about $10,000. Wright bought them for a total of $2. Purdue had paid for the instruments, the University used them, and that information was advertised. Everyone benefited.

In 1957 the band put out a vinyl 12-inch LP album—the band's second record. It was a "Big Ten Salute" and contained two songs from each of the Big Ten schools. The Purdue band played from sheet music obtained from each of the other nine schools in the conference, so the music was authentic.

The record was picked up by radio stations all over the country and used as opening and closing music as well as to reintroduce shows after commercials breaks. It was also used in television broadcasts in later years. Wright employed a valuable tactic that had also been used by Purdue bands during the Emrick years: it pays to perform the other school's songs.

Anatomy of a Uniform

1920s

1930s

1940s

UNIFORM OF THE AL WRIGHT ERA

Plume marks the beginning of more showy attire

Two uniforms in one! The epaulets and chest emblem are removable to make a basic black coat for the Purdue Orchestra.

White gloves and spats added to make hands and feet more visible

1960s

1966

Today

An exploding cannon is a fun effect that has been featured in band shows in various eras, pictured here in the 1970s.

In the fall of 1958, Wright and the Purdue band introduced new uniforms. These would come to be used as models for band uniforms all over the country. It was the first complete change in uniforms since Emrick had retired. It was the first time in its history that the band adopted non-military uniforms.

Part of the uniform problem for Wright had been the dual purposes of his bands. His marching band needed snappy uniforms to match its performances, and his symphonic band needed a more dignified, concert look, so he created a uniform that could fulfill both needs.

The key was removable parts.

The marching band uniform was black with gold accompaniments including a shoulder and sleeve epaulet and chest emblem. The chest emblem was gold and bore an interlocking "PU" signature.

However, when the symphonic band used the same uniforms, the sleeve epaulet and the chest emblem were removed, leaving a basic black uniform featuring a coat with a high collar. That uniform for the band remained until replaced by black tails.

Throughout the 1960s, Wright kept the traditions going. The band grew in size to more than four hundred members. The "World's Largest Drum" was maintained (read more about the drum in chapter six). A continuous line of Golden Girls stretched forward from 1954 (read more about the Golden Girls in chapter five). There were also fabulous trips to South American, Europe, Canada, and Iceland (read more about the band trips in chapter nine).

Bill Kisinger was a Purdue assistant band director hired by Wright in 1969.

"The Al Wright style was band pageantry," Kisinger said. "It used picture formations, and to get from one picture to the next, each rank would go around in circles and curly lines. It looked like a big plate of worms and then zap, another picture. Then a big plate of worms again and then zap, another picture."

Harold Walters did most of the arrangements, often on short notice. On Sunday Wright would call and tell him what he wanted for his next halftime show.

"He could work very fast," Wright said. "Over the years he wrote two million notes for me and not one of them was wrong."

Wright had a concept of what kind of marching the group would do on the field well before fall arrived, but he couldn't block out the formations until band camp when they knew how many marchers were available. Wright used toy soldiers to plot his halftime shows.

Purdue was the first Big Ten band to carry the colors of all the conferences' universities, as pictured here in 1975.

Drumline at Liberty Bowl in Memphis, Tennessee, in 1980.

One of Wright's most inspirational performances with the "All-American" Marching Band came not inside, but outside a football stadium. It exemplified the spirit of the band and the respect band members had for Wright.

In 1980 Purdue went to the Liberty Bowl in Memphis, Tennessee. The band members stayed in one of the taller hotels in the city, about twelve floors. More than four hundred Purdue band members were all put in rooms on the street side of the hotel.

The rooms had beautiful windows, but no one spent much time looking out them before the football game because of the band's heavy practice schedule.

Come game day, the band performed its shows, the football team won, and the band members went back to their hotel exhausted but fired up with excitement. What better way to express themselves than getting out their instruments and playing? With several people playing brass instruments in each of the small rooms, it became too noisy inside, so they moved to the windows and opened them.

Up and down the side of the hotel they tooted their horns, creating a horrible racket, with each of the hundreds of musician playing a different song.

By chance, Wright was walking out of the hotel at the time, and when he got across the street he looked up to see what the commotion was all about.

At the same time, the band members saw their director, sensed they might be making enough noise to shake the nerves of all of Memphis inhabitants, and they stopped. They were all silently looking down at Wright, wondering what he would say. Were they in trouble?

Wright didn't say a word. He just raised his arms and held his hands above his head. That was all the band members needed to see. They didn't need words. They knew what that meant.

They raised their instruments to the ready position. When Wright's arms dropped, giving them the command to begin, they didn't need to be told what song to play.

They performed "Hail Purdue" for the whole town to hear—the band stretched out up and down the side of the hotel, the band director on the other side of the street commanding the performance.

It was the last time before his retirement and elevation to emeritus status that Wright would direct the "All-American" Marching Band in conjunction with a football game.

And his band never played better.

CHAPTER FOUR

FOLLOWING THE "ALL-AMERICAN" PATH OF GREATNESS

Moffit, Kisinger, Leppla, and Gephart

Previous page: Bill Kisinger at the Capitol One Bowl 2000.

Colorful costumes seen during the Wright era (similar to the one pictured above) disappeared when Bill Moffit introduced his "Patterns of Motion" marching style.

"The thing I love about Purdue is the students. I'm always impressed at what good quality people they are. I'm never disappointed in them, and that's why I love working here."

—*Purdue University Director of Bands Jay Gephart*

People often talk about the enthusiasm of students in the Purdue "All-American" Marching Band. They clearly love being part of this great, historic musical organization.

It might be less apparent when audience members see them marching down the street alongside the band, or standing on ladders conducting during halftime shows, but the leaders of the band love what they are doing, too.

And during 125 years of history, everyone who has directed the Purdue "All-American" Marching Band will agree: it is the students that make it such a wonderful experience.

Two men—Paul Spotts Emrick and Al G. Wright—dominate the history of bands at Purdue University for a combined seventy-six years—from 1905 until 1981.

They served as marching band directors and also conducted symphony bands and other groups as needed. They both held the title "Director of Bands."

When Wright retired in 1981, J. Richard Dunscomb became director of bands, and a long-standing tradition was changed. Dunscomb decided to find someone else to lead the marching band.

Dunscomb received his degrees from Millikin University in Decatur, Illinois, taught in public schools for twelve years, and was teaching at Central High School in Champaign when he was hired by Purdue in 1974. He worked with various bands and was recruited to focus on jazz.

A small man with a big sense of humor, Moffit was constantly throwing out puns.

"Because of my philosophy of searching for a quality education for the students, I decided not to do the marching band," he said. "I knew I could hire someone to do that job who already had a national reputation, who would uphold the traditions, and yet take off in some new directions. I knew the job of administration would be very heavy. And, I loved the jazz groups, and I didn't want to give those up."

Following a national search, Dunscomb hired William Moffit, director of the University of Houston Marching Band.

In Moffit, the "All-American" band received more than a director. He was also an arranger. At the time of his death in 2008, he had published 450 band arrangements that had sold more than one million copies. One of his most popular arrangements continues to be the "Star Spangled Banner."

Before arriving at Purdue, Moffit had developed a marching style called "Patterns of Motion." It featured band members in constantly changing kaleidoscopic patterns on the field. Based on a four-person squad system, "Patterns in

Motions" was used by bands through the nation and led to many changes in marching band style.

In addition to his skills as an arranger, his marching style, and national reputation, Moffit brought one more important asset to Purdue: unbridled enthusiasm.

On the day of his first interview with the Lafayette news media, he sat in Dunscomb's office. Instead of sitting back in his chair, he turned it around and sat with the back of the chair resting near his chin. Every time he talked about his plans at Purdue, he stood up and talked faster and faster.

His speech included words like "exciting," "creative," and "fresh." That enthusiasm became the theme of the bands under his direction. It was contagious, and Moffit knew how to spread the attitude.

Moffit was fascinated by bands all his life. He saw his first parade as a toddler in North Canton, Ohio. He viewed it through the legs of the adults, but he remembered that day into adulthood.

When he first heard a circus calliope, he went immediately to the high school band director and asked to perform in the band. To test their potential, all new students had to study a pre-band instrument. After a year, when the band director asked Moffit what instrument he would really like to play, he went home and talked it over with his family. "Why don't you play the trombone, Bill?" his uncle asked. "The trombone players march right in front behind the majorettes."

He took the advice and appeared at the front of the band.

Moffit played and arranged for bands in the U.S. Coast Guard during World War II. He was the first teenager to play with the Coast Guard Jazz Band.

Two Moffit variations of the Block "P," which were popular during his tenure with the band.

Right: Frank Stubbs, orchestra director and department head.

After the war, he graduated cum laude from Baldwin-Wallace College in Berea, Ohio, in 1950. He received his master's degree from the University of Michigan. Moffit taught band in public schools and was named marching band director at Michigan State University from 1959 to 1968. In 1968 he went to the University of Houston and remained there until 1981, when he came to Purdue.

"I thought Purdue had perhaps the greatest opportunity for marching band performances in the country," Moffit said. "With no school of music, the students are in the band because they want to be in the band. The size of the band was already here, and that showed me there was no limit as far as size goes. What I tried to do when I came [to Purdue] was work with the quality of the musicians. Because we don't have a school of music, a lot of the students don't have time to practice on their own. So I created musical calisthenics as part of our daily warm up to help them develop and refine and maintain their excellent playing skills."

Moffit used a squad system of marching in which each squad had its own series of maneuvers. "It looked like sticks going from one formation to the next," said Bill Kisinger, who worked as an assistant band director under Moffit. "Where Al Wright's style stressed what the formation looked like in the end, Bill Moffit's style was more concerned with how you get to that end."

In addition to using his own arrangements and marching patterns, Moffit added more elements to the halftime shows, elements that quickly became traditions. He added an additional "P" to the "Block 'P'" formation on the football field so that a "P" faced each side of the stadium. He brought out huge American and Indiana flags for pregame ceremonies. He found a loud train whistle, placed it atop the scoreboard, and it let out a blast after every touchdown.

He brought in fanfare trumpets and used them in the flag-raising ceremony. The Purdue "All-American" Marching Band and Moffit quickly became famous for those trumpets, and Moffit was asked to write fanfares for the 1984 Summer Olympics in Los Angeles. He was invited to direct the fanfare trumpets during the spectacular opening festivities. Several Purdue fanfare trumpet players went with him.

"Being in the band should be a positive life experience," Moffit said. "It's an example of citizenship; people working together to achieve a common good. The people in the band work hard on their performance, and then they give it away at no cost to everyone who can hear it and see it."

While Moffit was adding the new, he was using the old—old uniforms. The uniforms he inherited dated back to the Rose Bowl from 1968 and were pushing twenty years old by the time they were replaced late in the 1985 football season.

The band department wanted to maintain three elements from the old uniforms introduced by Wright. They wanted to continue the block "P," the "Purdue" written in script, and the "All-American" band patch. They ended up selecting new

J. Richard Dunscomb, who served as director of the Purdue Bands Department and director of the Jazz Band, developed a high profile for the jazz program.

Clockwise from top left:

Only rarely does the Purdue band abandon its uniforms for a performance, but they did for the Western Michigan game in 1993.

Parading through fans to Ross-Ade Stadium in 2000.

Souvenir towels salute senior quarterback Drew Brees in 2000. Brees would go on to become a Super Bowl MVP.

For several years, groups of "Band Ambassadors" took programs to elmentary schools, encouraging kids to try different instruments and to march.

Traditions

Clockwise from top left:

The drum major breakdown is a traditional ending to game day, pictured here in 2001.

Band members in Halloween costumes, a practice tradition on October 31.

Gray wool jackets decorated with embroidered marching band memories are a continuing tradition.

Band senior hits the "World's Largest Drum." In the 1990s, it became a tradition for graduating seniors to hit the drum in Ross-Ade Stadium at the final home game of their senior year. They cannot hit it at any other time.

Facing page: Tuba Cadence, a ritual going back decades, calls upon band members to stop on their post-game march to Hovde Hall, break ranks, and commiserate about their level of exhaustion.

The band presents their traditional flag ceremony in Ross-Ade Stadium in the wake of September 11, 2001.

uniforms almost identical in look to the old ones but without detachable parts. Those uniforms were still in use on the 125th anniversary of Purdue University Bands.

In 1988, the year he retired from Purdue, the Indiana General Assembly named Moffit "Indiana's Music Arranger Laureate" and the Purdue Board of Trustees awarded him the title of "Professor of Bands Emeritus."

Dunscomb also left Purdue in 1988 and was succeeded by Frank Stubbs as director of bands.

Wright hired Stubbs in 1978 as orchestra director. He came from his own alma mater, Stetson University, in DeLand, Florida, where he held the title director of bands. He received his master's degree from Ithaca College in New York and studied at Emory University in Atlanta before returning to Stetson.

Stubbs was excited about working at Purdue with students who excelled in subjects like math, engineering, and science, rather than music.

"When I was at Stetson one of my responsibilities was recruiting," he said. "We'd go out and listen to someone play the violin, and very often when we got to the bottom line, they wanted to talk about our engineering school or our physics school. We found that a lot of very fine musicians were going to scientific schools."

Like Dunscomb, Stubbs did not direct the marching band. In 1988 the job was handled by assistant directors Kisinger and Joe Manfredo while a national search was conducted for Moffit's replacement.

Originally from Calumet City, Illinois, Manfredo received a bachelor's degree in music education and a Master of Arts degree in conducting from Eastern Illinois University. He earned a Doctorate in Music Education from the University of Illinois where he went after leaving Purdue.

Kisinger arrived at Purdue in 1969, following six years of teaching at public high schools. He was a native of Champaign, Illinois, where his father was marching band director at the University of Illinois.

For thirty-seven years Kisinger's passion for music and Purdue helped shape Purdue University Bands. During his career, he worked with six of the seven people other than himself who have directed the "All-American" Marching Band in its first 125 years of history—everyone but Emrick. Kisinger retired in 2006, second in longevity only to Emrick.

Like Emrick and Wright, Kisinger became a legend at Purdue, and he is the only director who is included in the band's official cheer (read more about the cheer in chapter ten).

"I loved the kids at Purdue," Kisinger said. "Purdue kids are genuine and I really enjoyed working with them. And I love Big Ten football. My mother is buried across the street from the University of Illinois stadium. I looked at a lot of other jobs over the years. But I didn't like the feel of those campuses like I loved Purdue."

Kisinger designed shows for a number of "All-American" band directors, a job that changed a lot over the years. When he worked with Wright, they used toy soldiers and charts. By the late twentieth century, it was all being done on computers. "That made everything fast," he said.

Designing marching band shows is very difficult. For example, to make a letter formed by the band on a football field look normal to the people sitting in the stands at Ross-Ade, it has to be three times as tall as it is wide. Computers enable designers to see the show exactly as it will look from each sideline and the end zones.

Students loved Kisinger as much as he loved them.

He listed among his favorite moments seeing a student struggle to accomplish a task and finally succeeding. He also enjoyed:

Hats worn backward signify a Big Ten victory, as shown by Bill Kisinger in this 2005 image. He served thirty-seven years as assistant director, from 1969–2006.

Drumline gets in the spirit of Christmas at the annual Lafayette Christmas Parade. Traditionally, the band precedes Santa.

Having the band perform well under adverse weather conditions. Having a lousy final rehearsal and then taking it to the next level and nailing the performance in the stadium. Sometimes I like to use some SAT words while giving instruction. If a student asks what that means, sometimes I answer and sometimes I say look it up in a dictionary. The next rehearsal a student reports to rehearsal with a dictionary in hand. That's when you know you are getting to them.

While the primary focus of our bands is preparation for performance and striving for excellence, I hope that my students developed a sense of what constitutes good music and a desire to continue with music in their adult lives through participation in bands, chamber ensembles, as connoisseurs of music at concerts, shows, and by purchasing recordings of quality music. It is interesting to note that band alumni often tell me that the nonmusical aspects [being punctual, leadership opportunities, being prepared, being flexible when traveling, etc.] of participating in band prepared them to become successful in their chosen career. It is common for an alumnus to say 'not a day goes by in my career that I don't draw upon my band experience to perform better in my job.'

In 1989 David Leppla was hired as director of the "All-American" Marching Band, the fourth individual to hold that position in the band's history. Before coming to Purdue, Leppla spent thirteen years as instrumental music director in the public and parochial schools of Ohio. Leppla received his bachelor's degree from the University of Dayton and his master's and doctorate from The Ohio State University, where he was a member of the marching band staff.

When the job at Purdue opened, he had just completed his PhD and did not think he had a chance at the position, but he was encouraged to try by an advisor and mentor.

"I was familiar with the Big Ten, and I knew that Purdue was one of the best marching bands in the country," Leppla said. "Purdue had developed a wonderful reputation under Al Wright and Bill Moffit. I was just really astounded to be able to come out of a PhD program and step into a band with the history and luster that Purdue had."

Shortly after Leppla arrived, Stubbs left to lead the Plymouth Music Series in Minneapolis, Minnesota, and Leppla was named director of bands at Purdue.

When he took over the marching band, Leppla decided against bringing any of the traditions from Ohio State to West Lafayette. He wanted to build on the traditions at Purdue.

"If you study the top collegiate programs in the country, the ones that are really strong have a good sense of tradition—

Coming Home

Clockwise from top left:

Martin and Patty Jischke lead parade of Golden Girls at 50th reunion in 2004.

Alumni band members execute traditional run-in to Elliott Hall at Homecoming 2009.

During Homecoming 2007, the band and alumni create the "World's Largest Block 'P'" on the formation's 100th anniversary.

WORLD'S LARGEST

Purdue President Steven Beering poses with David Leppla, the fourth marching band director and department head, who served from 1988–2006.

the students believe in them and the staff believes in them," Leppla said. "You build a program around those traditions."

Several traditions did change with the times and one more was added—the postgame concert at the fountain in front of Hovde Hall.

The "Fountain Concert" was created for two reasons. First, the National Association of Intercollegiate Athletics wanted to use postgame time at Ross-Ade Stadium to broadcast the coach's interview; and second, the University decided to end the band's tradition of running into Elliott Hall of Music at the end of a long football Saturday.

The coach's interview cut short the band's postgame performances at Ross-Ade. At the time, the University had just completed the fountain in front of Hovde Hall.

"We were wondering if we could create a following for a postgame performance away from the stadium," Leppla said. "One day Bill Kisinger and I got some lunch, and we sat on the stairs at Hovde, and we talked about how this would work."

Meanwhile, Stubbs had also informed Leppla that a long-standing tradition of band members running through the doors to Elliott Hall of Music in sections would have to stop.

"Frank said the decision had been made that the run-in was unsafe," Leppla said. "It had been a huge tradition. But we had to do something different."

The decision was made to put the audience on the steps of Hovde Hall. The band would play around the fountain and would depart for Elliott Hall of Music in sections at the end of the performance.

Leppla remembers marching out of Ross-Ade toward the first concert around the fountain and wondering if anyone would be there.

"We had a pretty good crowd," he said. And it has continued to be a popular feature on game days.

Leppla said that among the many things that make the Purdue "All-American" Marching Band great, one of the most important is the student leadership.

"The students are involved in planning, making decisions, teaching, and leadership," he said. "With four hundred people in the band, you can't make that work unless you have students who believe in what they're doing and want to work hard. I was blessed to have phenomenal student leaders. They deserve the credit for making things work."

Under Leppla's leadership, in 1995 the band was awarded the prestigious Sudler Trophy. It is referred to as the Heisman Trophy for marching bands and can only be won once. The selection of each year's trophy recipient is based upon musicality, precision, and overall excellence.

Previous page: Football team sings "Hail Purdue" with the band and Drum Major Stephanie Swierczek following a victory over Western Michigan University in 2002.

Ross-Ade crowd and band salute Purdue astronaut Jerry Ross, escorted by Goldduster Sheenah Johnson, at Minnesota University game in 2002.

Present Day Formations

As the Purdue "All-American" Marching Band moved into the twenty-first century, it continued the tradition of creating interesting and beautiful pictures on the field—among them a stylized flower, an outline of the United States, and a trumpet with notes floating out of its bell.

Left: The first African American drum major was Cherrie Lemon, who was selected in 2010.

Right: Purdue's first female drum major (at right) Anne Woods from Fort Wayne, Indiana, led the band in 1991–1992. Her fellow drum major is Ian Hendrix.

It was also during the Leppla era that the first woman became a drum major. Even though women had been part of the instrumental block since 1974, it wasn't until 1991 that Anne Woods, of Fort Wayne, Indiana, became the first female drum major. In 2010 another first took place when Cherrie Lemon, of St. Louis, Missouri, became the first African American drum major.

Leppla retired at the end of June, 2006 and was replaced as director of bands and director of the "All-American" Marching Band by Jay S. Gephart.

Gephart joined the Purdue band faculty in the fall of 1995 after having completed twelve years as a public school band director. In July 2001 he was promoted to the rank of associate professor with tenure, and in November 2006 he became director of university bands. In addition to directing the "All-American" Marching Band, Gephart initially served as the music director for the Purdue Symphony Orchestra.

He received a Bachelor of Music Education Degree with Distinction from Indiana University in 1983, and a Master of Music Degree in Performance with High Distinction from Indiana University in 1988. His first instrument was the clarinet, but he later switched to the tuba.

During his career, Gephart has conducted All-State Bands in Indiana and Arkansas and served in Chicago as a clinician at the Midwest Clinic, an International Band and Orchestra Conference. In 1997 he was selected to conduct the music camp honor band for the Australian Department of Education in the northern region of Queensland. He has been the recipient of many awards and honors including the Indiana Outstanding Bandmaster Award and the Purdue New Professional Award.

Gephart grew up in Montgomery County, just south of West Lafayette. Although he didn't attend Purdue as a student, coming to the University was like returning home for him. He had known about the Purdue University Bands his entire life, and many of his friends graduated from the West Lafayette campus.

His first decision as director of bands was to take leadership of the "All-American" Marching Band.

"I decided it was important for me to take over the reigns of the 'All-American' Marching Band," he said. "It's an important part of tradition at Purdue that the director of bands directs the marching band. You don't see this in other bands around the country, but it's an in important part of our history."

Clockwise from top left:

Boiler Brass sports "Paint Crew" shirts and bumblebee knee socks in Matt Painter basketball era.

Gold & Black Sound brings back Bill Moffit tradition of "Tuba Hail" for women's basketball games during the 2000s.

Boiler Brass in 2003.

Volleyball Band Hawaiian Night in 2001.

Clockwise from top left:

Telling a story through a tune has been a trademark of the Purdue band's halftime show style.

Patriotic salute during 2009 halftime show.

The drumline.

Gephart is impressed with the students who carry on the traditions and play a key role in band leadership. He said:

> *What we attract at Purdue is high-end, top students, who because of the nature of the discipline they study, have to be self disciplined. Otherwise they wouldn't be successful. It's a given that students at Purdue will have a high GPA. That's not just because they're born intelligent. They work very hard. In our band program, we reap the benefits of these hard working students.*
>
> *The students fascinate me. They're interested in disciplines I have no clue about, and I'm awed at their understanding of so many things. They all have a passion for marching bands, and this is not the case at all universities where music majors are required to take marching to graduate.*
>
> *Amateur is defined as someone who does something for the love of it. That's our students. There is something very healthy about this experience at Purdue. Our students can take this love they have for music and translate it into something over a lifetime.*
>
> *Another reason I love Purdue is the whole essence of what it means to be part of the band family. It's inconceivable to think of a university like Purdue without a band program. If this department ceased to exist, Purdue students who love music and marching would find one another, and they would create a band, just like they did at the beginning of our history.*

Left: Directors exchange gifts following a joint concert, which combined student musicians from Purdue and China in 2008. The Chinese band director received a Purdue "All-American" Marching Band jacket and plumed hat.

Right: Jay Gephart (center) serves as the fifth Purdue "All-American" Marching Band director and department head (2006–present), with Pam Nave and Max Jones serving as marching assistants.

Band members create Block "P" in 2010 under the leadership of Jay Gephart.

CHAPTER FIVE

WOMEN IN THE BAND

Majorettes to Golden Girls and Beyond

Previous page: Golden Girl MerrieBeth Cox (2008–) performs.

Below: Golden Girl trading cards are a popular item. Pictured is the 24th Golden Girl Christy Jayne Stallings.

Golden: lustrous; exceptionally valuable, radiant; full of happiness; highly talented.

To be golden is to be the best, and to be Golden Girl at Purdue University is the ambition of countless girls and young women throughout the United States.

They begin preparing when they are five or six years old and even younger. They practice endless hours with their batons and dream about being outfitted in gold, performing in a football stadium surrounded by 63,000 people, with a national television audience tuned in.

Only twenty-seven young women have fulfilled that dream during the first 125 years of Purdue Bands. Others sought different featured positions with the "All-American" Marching Band: they have performed as Girl in Black or a Silver Twin. They have taken part in a twirling line, the Goldusters Dance Team, or the Golden Silks Color Guard. Many more women have marched and played an instrument in the band.

Whatever role these women accept, the experience is unforgettable, and it is an experience that has only been available for a relatively short period of time.

The involvement of women in the band program dates back to the late 1930s and early 1940s but was very limited in those early days. They carried flags. Some were majorettes. Generally, they were not allowed to play instruments and march. In fact, it was not until the early 1970s that women were widely accepted into the block band as musicians and marchers.

Among those who entered Purdue in the fall of 1974 was Ann Ferris, who graduated from West Lafayette High School, played in the marching band there, and never had a second thought about what she would do when she entered Purdue. She would be part of the band. And she was.

"It was fairly new ground at the time," Ferris said. "I believe it was the second year that women were allowed to march in what was called the block. I didn't realize at the time it was rather historic. It didn't seem unusual. I didn't feel like it was different. It was a great experience."

Ferris played clarinet and had to pull her hair up under her band cap. It was a time when numerous opportunities became available very suddenly for women and society was changing quickly—too quickly for some, and not fast enough for others.

The transition happened so naturally, it is hard to imagine the many years it took to reach the point where Ferris and other young women were allowed to march in a band.

Through much of the 1960s, many football stadiums had policies that no women were allowed on the field. Exceptions were made for baton twirlers. Even Gladys Wright, the wife of Director of Bands Al Wright, once had to sneak onto the Notre Dame Stadium field covered by a cape so no one could see that she was a woman.

When Paul Spotts Emrick opened up his military band to women in 1939, the opening was narrow. His idea of a band was a military unit—a precision team—and women didn't fit into his concept.

Emrick's changing policy was part of a growing feeling that there weren't enough activities and opportunities for young women on campus.

In Emrick's band, women could march and twirl, but they could not play an instrument with the band. Female musicians were restricted to a symphony band.

Emrick's first majorettes performed in 1939: Eleanor Poor, of Etna Glen, Ohio, and Barbara Lohmmen, of Cleveland Heights, Ohio. The majorettes were popular, and in 1941

Emrick was working on a plan for the majorette program that would make it even more successful.

He had attended football games at Jefferson High School in Lafayette, and had come across twins named Mary and Marjorie Vaughan. They created a sensation as Jefferson's majorettes.

The Jefferson band director had come up with the idea of twirling twins and approached the girls' father, prominent Lafayette attorney and judge Charles Vaughan. Mary and Marjorie didn't even know how to twirl, but their father said if they were willing to learn, it was fine with him.

The first time the twins marched with the high school band during halftime of a football game, the students ran down out of the stands and stood along the edge of the field, walking up and down the sidelines with the girls. Then they carried Mary and Marjorie off the field like football heroes.

Emrick thought this was just the thing for his Purdue band in the early 1940s. The twins attended Purdue, and when they joined the band, they received almost as enthusiastic a response as they had received at Jefferson High School. People loved them. They became the first twirlers at Purdue to gain national fame, through photographs in *Life* magazine.

Below: Eleanor Poor (left) and Barbara Lohmmen became the first majorettes with the band in the fall of 1939.

Left: Twins Mary and Marjorie Vaughan brought national fame to Purdue's majorette corps when they were featured in *Life* magazine, 1943.

They received letters from admirers from all over the country. They received so much mail that the Lafayette Post Office called and asked them to pick it up themselves.

The Vaughan twins graduated, but the majorette tradition continued with Donna Jeanne Kelling, Wanda Evans, Phyllis Pesha, Juanita Fowler, Carolyn Marshall, and Jane Estegren.

Still, when it came to featured roles, the most famous twirler with the band in the 1940s was a male—Nick Michalares, a national champion who had also served four years in the Navy during the war in the Pacific Theater.

The majorettes in the band in the late 1940s wore pants. Their uniforms were the same that Eleanor Poor and Barbara Lohmmen had worn in 1939—canary yellow, trimmed in black.

The last year the band's majorettes would be dressed in trousers, 1951.

The uniforms were heavy and uncomfortable during the early hot Saturdays of the football season and at the Indianapolis Motor Speedway at the end of May.

Anita "Teedee" Carley was still a student at Jefferson High School when she twirled for Purdue. She remembered her desire to get rid of the hot uniforms and wear skirts, which were becoming more popular for majorettes at other universities.

According to the band photographer of the 1940s, Dave Chambers, it was Wilbur Shaw, of the Indianapolis Motor Speedway, who finally changed the image of women in the Purdue "All-American" Marching Band. As a driver, Shaw won the Indianapolis 500 race three times, in 1937, 1939, and 1940. From 1945 until his death in 1954, he was president of the Indianapolis Motor Speedway.

"At a meeting before the race in 1951, Shaw suggested to the band officers that they might want to get the girls cooler uniforms and something the public would like a little more," Chambers said. "The girls had wanted to do just that for some time, but [Emrick] wouldn't hold still for it because it wasn't military. But when Wilbur Shaw wanted it, that was fine, because [Emrick] loved Wilbur Shaw. He'd go a long way to do whatever Wilbur Shaw wanted."

The majorettes designed the skirt uniforms, which were predominantly white with gold and black trim and a crest on the front with an interlocking "PU." They wore the outfits for the first time at the Indianapolis 500 in 1951.

"And from that time on, Emrick never let us wear pants again," Riehle said.

Those same skirts were in use when Al Wright came to Purdue, replacing the legendary Emrick. In the summer of 1954 he was preparing to enter his first football season conducting the marching band, the most publicly visible part of his job.

By the fall of 1953, these majorettes had already spent one year in skirts. The corps continued to grow in the years ahead.

The thirty-eight-year-old band director, who had come to Purdue from a prominent position in a Florida high school, was looking for ways to put his own mark on the program—to accomplish a goal that President Frederick Hovde had suggested: Make some changes.

Wright had an enormous talent for taking the best of what was available and making it even better, as well as adding his own innovative ideas. He made one of his first big moves during a high school band camp in Colorado the summer before the 1954 fall season.

Wright had been going to this camp for a number of years while he served as director of bands at Miami High School. During previous years he had met a high school

Golden Girl Juanita Carpenter, 1954–1956.

girl, a baton twirler named Juanita Carpenter. She was a good twirler with all-American good looks, who could move naturally and spontaneously, who could dance and twirl in front of a crowd and at the front of a band.

Wright had noticed her in years past, but during the 1954 summer he took a particular interest, as did his wife, Gladys, who was also a band director and was working at the camp.

Carpenter came from a small town in Colorado—Lamar, population eight thousand. Everything about her was perfect for a role at Purdue in West Lafayette. Wright saw in her qualities that people in Indiana would love—a girl who looked and acted the way a father would like his daughter to look and act. She was the kind of girl that turned the heads of college boys.

Carpenter, however, wanted to study drama and go into the entertainment business. She was already enrolled at the University of Denver, her father's alma mater. She had a small scholarship there, and the university had an excellent school of drama.

Al and Gladys Wright thought they had a better offer for Carpenter and they both discussed it with her.

"I have this new job at Purdue," Wright told the young girl. "Why don't you come with me and be a solo twirler with the band?"

There was no scholarship to offer, and Wright was unsure if she would accept. Yet there was also no question in Carpenter's mind about what she wanted to do.

"For a kid who grew up in a ranch town in Colorado, getting asked to go to Purdue was pretty heady stuff," she said. "The only time we saw Big Ten universities was on newsreels."

She twisted arms at home, her parents relented, and a few weeks later Carpenter found herself in West Lafayette.

Before she arrived, however, she decided to take a few tips from a twirling instructor at the band camp. The instructor was from California, so naturally Carpenter figured she knew just about everything about putting on an impressive show.

"She just had a flair about her," Carpenter said. "She had so much showmanship. And then she related to me how she had been so plain. But she had bleached her hair platinum blonde, and she had this outfit that was solid silver, and she was my idol."

Carpenter got a sequined twirling outfit, and a girlfriend at camp helped bleach her already blonde hair even blonder.

"But we got hold of the wrong stuff, and we left it on too long," Carpenter said. "It came out too silver, and some of the ends broke off. I had to cut my hair pretty short."

So Carpenter went off to Purdue with platinum blonde, short hair and the brand new sequin outfit with a short skirt that just happened to be gold.

Wright put Carpenter before the newspaper cameras as soon as she stepped foot on the University grounds. The plan was for her to be a featured, solo twirler. For the first football game she wore her gold outfit.

After that, the plan called for her to wear the color representing the school Purdue was playing. When Purdue played Notre Dame's Fighting Irish in 1954, Carpenter wore the school's favored green—even though the official Notre Dame colors are gold and blue. There were other colors for other schools on the schedule that year, but most of them were never used.

Wright had a better idea.

The star quarterback for the Purdue team that year was Len Dawson, a young man the press had dubbed the "Golden Boy." With Carpenter's platinum blonde hair and the gold outfit, she looked the part of a "Golden Girl," and Wright's wife urged him to call his featured twirler just that, which the news media accepted wholeheartedly.

She never wore any other color than gold again. A tradition was born. However, this was more than a tradition for a university. For Carpenter, personally, it was a golden time of her life.

During an interview in the mid-1980s she said she could still feel the tingle she had experienced when she first walked into Ross-Ade Stadium filled with many thousands more people than lived in her entire hometown. She loved to perform and twirl and strut and dance and smile at the people in the stands.

"I wanted to go up and embrace everybody up there," she said. "I received fan mail. I remember receiving a cigarette once in the mail. Some guy wanted me to smoke it and return it to him through the mail. I absolutely loved what I was doing. To me, this is what college was."

Golden Girl Sandra Hutchison, 1956–1958.

It was, of course, tough at times, too. The discipline was strict. The band performed no matter what the weather.

Wright told her on cold days he didn't want her legs to turn blue. That was before the days of panty hose, so she had to find some other way to keep warm. She couldn't find anything. So if the girls with the band couldn't have warm legs, at least they could keep them from turning blue by using facial makeup.

Golden Girls Through the Ages

Clockwise from top:

Golden Girl Reunion, 2004

Susan Fron, 1979–1982

Linda Hughes, 1973–1976

Selita Sue Smith, 1969–1973

Facing page:

Alisha Bane, 1994–1995

Ann Loppnow, 1996–2000

Valerie Ludwick, 1983–1987

"But then if you got wet at all, you got streaks down your legs, and we were constantly running off to the girls' room to fix our makeup on our legs," Carpenter said.

Cold was the problem part of the time. Heat was the problem at other times.

"I remember sometimes at the [Indianapolis 500] it would be so hot and humid," Carpenter said. "Al Wright didn't want us to pass out. We had ammonia capsules to breathe if we started to feel faint."

Carpenter also had another problem, and it was a familiar problem to every young student who leaves home and goes off to college: the college diet.

"The dorm food was awfully starchy, and I would come in from band practice and eat like a horse," Carpenter said.

So Wright started to weigh her to keep her figure where it had been when she came to Purdue. In addition to Carpenter, he had all the twirlers in the band weighed. It was a tradition that continued for many years to follow.

For Carpenter, it all was great fun and everything she had expected. However, there were also some problems.

Not everyone approved of her costume, her hair, or her performances with the band. Her costume was conservative compared to what would come later. Her gold sequin suit featured a short skirt. She had a high collar, and on cold days she even wore long sleeves. She wore a top hat with a plume and white boots with tassels—all standard enough for majorettes of the day.

However, what might have been routine dress for a majorette in Miami or Los Angeles was not routine in Indiana, where women in the band only five years earlier had been forced to wear long slacks and waistcoats.

Carpenter always remembered what her father told her: "If you want your place in the sun, you've got to expect to get burned a little." She learned to take the criticism as gracefully as possible, because she did love her place in the sun.

"I hurt a little inside, but I never let anyone know it," she said.

She was the only featured twirler in the Big Ten that was female, but she had to follow Wright's rules just like everyone else. Up late bleaching her hair before the Purdue versus Indiana University game one year, she overslept. True to his rule, Wright told the buses to leave for the Bloomington without the Golden Girl.

Later, the big bass drum crew told Wright that they had to go back, that they had forgotten something. They didn't tell Wright that they were going back for Carpenter, but he probably realized the ruse quickly. She got to the game in time, but received demerits from Wright for missing the bus.

Juanita Carpenter passed away on Christmas Day, 2009, in San Diego, California at the age of seventy-three.

The Golden Girl title became a moveable crown. When Dawson left Purdue and went on to professional football and eventually the Hall of Fame, there was no Golden Boy to retain his title in Ross-Ade Stadium.

However, ever since Carpenter twirled at Ross-Ade Stadium in the fall of 1954, there has always been a Golden Girl at Purdue University.

Carpenter was replaced by Sandra Hutchinson, who twirled from 1956 to 1958 as the Golden Girl.

Next came Addie Darling. A young girl with fresh, Marilyn Monroe good looks, who loved to dance and perform before a crowd, she was an instant success at Purdue and everywhere she went. Addie Darling became Purdue's darling.

And then she wiggled. The Golden Girl has been famous nationwide ever since. It was the "Great Wiggle Controversy" that skyrocketed Wright's idea of a solo twirler in a gold suit into the national limelight.

Candice Nagle performs at a men's basketball game in Mackey Arena in 1987.

Wright found Darling in the same summer band camp where he had first met Carpenter. Her father was a high school band director in Manteca, California, and she had been marching and twirling all her life.

She entered Purdue at Wright's invitation and tried out for the Golden Girl position. She was the obvious choice.

On October 25, 1958, during her first season at Purdue, Darling went with the Purdue band to South Bend on a cold, rainy Saturday for the Notre Dame game. At halftime, when the band took the field, the game was tied at 7-7, but on this day the exploits of the band would overshadow the exploits of the football team.

Wright thought that Darling moved around too much when she performed on the field at halftimes. This time he had a solution for that. He got out a small platform and told her to dance on it.

The program that day featured a Purdue salute to the world, starting off, naturally, with Ireland and working its way through several continents. The program ended with "Hawaiian War Chant," and Darling, confined to a small area, moved what little she was able to move on the small platform: her hips. She did a twirling hula dance.

The response from the predominantly male crowd at Notre Dame Stadium was predictable. So was the response from the male television cameramen and directors. This was before the days of regional college football coverage, and a game on network television meant the game was broadcast coast to coast.

When the cameraman saw Darling wiggle, he went in for a close-up, and the wiggle was seen in living rooms all over America.

Most people loved the dance, which was innocent enough. However, two Purdue students, Julia Jackson and Mary Ellen Kennedy, quickly wrote a letter to the student

Addie Darling, 1958–1960

Twirling three batons was an easy feat for Golden Girl Holly Fehrman in December 1990.

newspaper, the *Exponent*, criticizing the wiggle.

"By this time everyone is well aware the university has a new Golden Girl," they wrote. "In fact, after last Saturday's exhibition on nationwide television, everyone in the country knows it. She not only walks and talks, but wiggles excessively."

It was a publicity gift made in heaven for Wright, and it had just the opposite effect the two girls had intended. When controversy arose over the Golden Girl's wiggle, it was too much for newspaper editors of the 1950s to pass up.

Tongues wagged about the wiggle in West Lafayette and throughout the country. Headlines blared: "Twirls vs. Wiggles," "Golden Girl Wiggle Has Campus Buzzing," "Hip, Hip Hooray."

The next question was, now that Darling had wiggled in South Bend, would she wiggle at home? Would she do it at Ross-Ade? Would President Frederick Hovde let her?

"Well," Hovde said, "some people can wiggle well, and I guess if they can do something good, they should be allowed to do it."

The headline writers and photo editors at newspapers around the country went at it again. "Encore! Golden Girl Will Wiggle Again," cheered the *Chicago Daily News* headline from October 31, 1958.

The wiggle controversy did more to give the Golden Girl national fame than any single incident before or after.

After the wiggle, wherever Darling went she received attention. And she went a lot of places. She, and all Golden Girls, have not only been a symbol of the band, but also are a symbol of the University. Darling was the first to take this role to its limits by making many personal appearances. She went to houseware shows, agricultural shows, 4-H shows, charity shows, almost everywhere she was asked to appear.

However, all that glitters is not gold. Darling's story ends in tragedy.

On November 25, 1960, she unexpectedly married, making her ineligible to continue as Golden Girl. She resigned from the band but continued to attend classes at Purdue, where her new husband was a student. She maintained contact with band members.

The following February she was rushed from her apartment to St. Elizabeth Hospital in Lafayette where she was admitted in "very critical condition." She was unconscious with a cerebral hemorrhage. Darling died the next day. She was twenty-one years old.

Her sister, Teddie Darling, came to Purdue following Addie's death.

Teddie Darling not only became the only girl to follow a sister as Golden Girl, but she became the only girl promised the position before she arrived at the University. As just a junior in high school, she already showed many of the talents her sister possessed.

Teddie Darling's appearance at Purdue in the fall of 1962 inadvertently led to another band tradition—the Girl in Black—not for Teddie, but for another young woman.

After the death of Addie Darling, there was not a permanent Golden Girl for the 1961 football season. Indeed, Wright decided to have guest Golden Girls, changing them each week. The first was Marianne Swenson, a sophomore from Elwood, Indiana. At the second game, the guest Golden Girl was June Ciampa, a freshman from Dearborn, Michigan.

Ciampa was a champion twirler who had set her sights on Purdue when she learned through newspaper stories that the Golden Girl position was open. She sent a resume and a picture of herself to Wright. He promptly returned the picture, saying she wasn't right.

However, Ciampa was determined. The first day of tryouts, Wright took one look at her performance and told her to sit down. Ciampa couldn't believe she had been rejected again.

Later, Wright told her she would be one of the guest Golden Girls that season. He told her to leave the group because he knew immediately that he wanted her. Wright had recognized her from her photo, and he also realized he had made a mistake in rejecting her before he had seen her twirl.

Ciampa was a big hit in her first performance as guest Golden Girl. The *Indianapolis News* ran five photographs of her above the masthead in the Monday, October 16, 1961 edition. "Guest Golden Girl Sparks Purdue's Halftime Show," the headline said.

There were other guest Golden Girls that year, including Rhetta Harper, a twirler imported from Texas to show Hoosiers the various styles of twirling from different parts of the country. The variety served to give Purdue's Golden Girl position more publicity in other parts of the country.

However, by the Indiana University versus Purdue game at the end of the season, it was Ciampa who was featured as the Golden Girl, and she kept that role when the band went to South America immediately after Christmas in 1961.

The next fall, in 1962, Teddie Darling came to Purdue. She was given the role of Golden Girl as promised, but Wright wanted to find a spot for Ciampa.

He dressed Ciampa in Purdue's other color, black, and had her perform as the "International Twirler." A Ross-Ade press box announcer was so taken by Ciampa's talent that he asked Wright, "Who is that girl in black"?

His comment led to the "International Twirler" title being dropped and replaced with the more obvious "Girl in Black." Several women held the Girl in Black position during the 1960s, but the first four-year Girl in Black was Lisa Ross, who graduated in 1979.

Her career in twirling was rooted in a serious childhood accident in her hometown of Tipton, Indiana. At the age of

June Ciampa, 1962, 1964–1965

Silver Twins Susan Johnson and Cyndy Love twirl in a bullring on the band's South American trip in 1978.

seven, Ross had multiple surgeries on her arm from a fall. Her doctor's advice was to enroll in some form of therapy that would be fun as well as instrumental in the rehabilitation of her arm.

"Thanks to twirling, the therapy was successful, and my fairy-tale life began," Ross said.

"When I arrived at Purdue, Al Wright saw my waist length, coal-black hair and knew that the Golden Girl position did not fit my persona," she said. "My style of twirling was that of dance, gymnastics, and jazz all rolled into one. Along with my passion to perform, I loved being allowed to mold the Girl in Black position into what it is today. My style brought something different to the Purdue band program. Four years later, after performing and teaching in fifteen countries, my Purdue education far exceeded the classroom," she said.

Throughout the 1963 football season, Teddie Darling and June Ciampa continued in the roles. Then, early in 1964, Teddie Darling resigned.

Wright needed someone immediately to be Golden Girl for a Carnaval de Quebéc appearance, and he had his backup. Ciampa can still remember him walking down the steps at Elliott Hall of Music that day.

"June," he said, "put on your gold costume."

Ciampa became one of the most popular of all the Golden Girls, performing in the featured spot until she graduated in 1965.

By this time the Purdue Golden Girl position was the top twirling job in the country. Wright received as many as four hundred contacts every year from young women interested in becoming the Golden Girl. His mail was filled with inquiries and offers. One interested twirler who wanted to be Golden Girl sent him a life-size picture of herself. An oil millionaire sent Wright a signed check with no amount written in. All Wright had to do was name the tycoon's daughter the Golden Girl at Purdue, and he could add his own number and zeros.

Many interesting Golden Girl stories exist. One of the stories was told in *Brian Piccolo . . . A Short Season*, written by his wife, Jeannie Morris. Piccolo was a popular Chicago Bears football player who died of cancer at the age of twenty-six. In the 1960s the team had a summer training camp at Saint Joseph's College in Rensselaer, Indiana.

In the book, Morris tells the story of Piccolo seeing a blond girl practicing her baton in her front yard in Rensselaer. One day he stopped and talked with her.

"I'm going to be going down to a Purdue game in a couple years and I plan to see you on the field at halftime," he said. "You will be Purdue's Golden Girl."

"It was all he had to say," his wife wrote. "You could tell from her face that being Purdue's Golden Girl had been her dream." The girl was Linda Hughes, and she was Purdue's Golden Girl from 1973-1976.

The "All-American" Marching Band is filled with tradition, but even traditions can be adjusted with time.

In 1995 Dawn Vardaman became Purdue's Golden Girl. She was a brunette, and Director of Bands David Leppla told her that she could keep her natural hair color.

"There was nothing in writing that said the Golden Girl had to be blonde," Leppla said.

In reality, twirlers who were not blonde when they were awarded the position during tryouts traditionally dyed their hair before football season began.

"Dawn came to my office and she said she didn't look good as a blonde and she wasn't comfortable as a blonde. She wanted to know if she had to dye her hair. I said absolutely not," Leppla commented.

The Golden Girl wasn't selected for the color of her hair, he said. She was selected because she was the best twirler.

"We were in a different era from when this started," Leppla said. "Times change, situations change."

In addition to the Golden Girl and Girl in Black, Wright also started the Silver Twins tradition. During the 1960s, twins Karon and Sharon Roeske applied to Purdue. They were twirlers.

"You couldn't turn down talent like that," Wright said. "The chance of finding twins that are twirlers is a million to one, so I named them the 'Silver Twins' and put them on the field. Then I started getting letters from mothers who told me they had twin daughters, and they'd be [at Purdue] in 1987 or 1991."

He called them "Silver Twins" because he already had a Golden Girl, and gold and silver go well together.

Ever since the Roeske girls came to Purdue, there have been Silver Twins in the marching band, but they were not always twins. Sometimes when no twins were available, sisters were used, and there have been times when coeds who weren't even related have been chosen as look-alikes and given the title. At other times there have been two sets of twins performing with the band.

Twelve of the twenty-one sets of Silver Twins have actually been twins. In 2004 when Morgan and Megan VonDielingen were selected for the position, it was the first time in more than a decade that identical twins had been featured as Silver Twins. At that time the department rededicated itself to honoring the original definition of the position and to filling it with twin sisters in the decades to come.

Purdue's first Silver Twins Karon and Sharon Roeske. Notice the autograph of President Harry Truman on bottom left of drum head (see chapter six).

Silver Twins

The concept of performing twins started in the 1960s under Al Wright. In Purdue's history up until 2011, twelve of the twenty-one sets of Silver Twins have actually been twin sisters, not merely look-alikes.

Clockwise from top left:

Erin Griffin and Alisha Stenger

Jane and Jean Gilbert

Morgan and Megan VonDielingen

Sara and Chellie Zou

The title of "International Twirler" was established in 1962. It was later replaced by the title "Girl in Black."

Clockwise from top left:

Krista Woodward

Dawn Vardaman

Lisa Ross

Tierney Brown dancing with drum major Dan Campbell

Goldusters

The Golduster Dance Team, established in 1980, tackles many different performing duties. The group delivers high-energy routines at football and basketball games.

Clockwise from top left:

Fringed red, white, and blue uniforms were worn by the Goldusters in the early 1980s. Here a group escorts astronaut Gene Cernan, the last man on the moon in 1969, onto the field of Ross-Ade Stadium.

Goldusters in fall 1987.

Shelley Hardesty dances in fall 2004.

Tedi Tzinares dances in front of the squad in late 2000s.

Left: Golden Silks Flag Corps performs in front of Hovde Hall in 2002.

Right: Golden Silks Flag Corps marches through Times Square with the band during Macy's Thanksgiving Day Parade in 2010.

During the late 1970s, the drum and bugle corps movement became very popular in high schools across America. The result was an increased interest in color guard and less interest in twirling.

The Purdue band directors decided to make the most out of the talents that were coming to the University. The dance team concept was becoming more popular in high schools as well, and girls wanted to participate in that type of group at Purdue, so a dance team, called the Goldusters, was started in 1980.

Immediately, half the twirlers dropped their batons and stepped into the dance line.

More than just a dance line or a pom-pom squad, the Goldusters Dance Team tackles many different performing duties as part of the "All-American" Marching Band. Jazz, rock and roll, Broadway, ballet, hip-hop, and even a touch of cheerleading complement the Goldusters' performances.

Besides football games, the Golduster Dance Team also performs in parades, stage shows, and at various sporting and community events.

Another change in band auxiliary units, brought on by the evolution of high school band programs, was the flag corps. In the late 1960s and early 1970s, members of the flag corps at Purdue were auxiliary marchers—backups who carried flags with ten-foot poles and waved them from side to side. As the 1970s progressed, high school students came to Purdue with more experience as flag carriers. The poles also decreased in size from ten feet to eight feet, and then by half-foot increments down to six feet.

As the poles decreased in length, the bearers were able to perform more nimbly with the flags. By the mid-1980s, a proficient flag corps of twenty-four to thirty-two young

Golden Silks Flag Corps performs in 1986.

women (plus alternates) marched with the band.

At the bands' 125th anniversary, the group was known as the Golden Silks Color Guard, and the group boasted both men and women in its membership list. In the spring semester, the team becomes a competitive Winter Guard in the Independent A class of the MidWest Color Guard Circuit.

Since 1999, former Golden Girl Alisha Bane Kuckartz has guided Purdue's auxiliary units, working closely with the twirlers and dancers. A Benton County native, she started twirling at the age of six after watching the Purdue band perform at a football game.

"It was really rewarding to be named Golden Girl [1994-1995] after having that goal for so long," she said. "And it was a great experience. It was a big accomplishment in my life."

As the owner of a private dance studio in West Lafayette, which also provides twirling lessons, Kuckartz works tirelessly to keep the sport alive and to help other young women fulfill their dreams.

She has seen the changing interests among young women coming to Purdue, and she said Purdue Bands has responded.

"In the Midwest, high school twirling is not as popular as it once was. But it remains popular in some areas, such as the South," she commented. "Through outreach appearances at national twirling events and increased recruiting efforts, Director of Bands Jay Gephart and I are working on specific strategies to make sure Purdue's rich twirling traditions continue into the future."

Although the physical characteristics of the band change, the experiences of being part of the exceptional group change very little. The enthusiasm that exuded from Juanita Carpenter's voice when she talked about being the first Golden Girl in 1954 is reflected in MerrieBeth Cox's voice in 2011,

Long-skirted flag attire was typical of the mid-1990s.

Goldduster Amber McDowell at the Michigan game in 2010.

Goldusters perform in the style of the Radio City Music Hall Rockettes in 2003.

and in voices of Golden Girls throughout time, like Valerie Ludwick, who held the position from 1983 to 1987.

"I spent four years in the band, and those were some of the happiest times of my life," Ludwick said. "I will always be [part of the band]. There will be other Golden Girls, but I'll always be the thirteenth Golden Girl. And all the experiences we as a band shared are going to go with me, wherever I go. They're a part of me now. They're with me in everything I do."

Golden Girls Through History

Juanita Carpenter, 1954–1956
Sandra Hutchinson, 1956–1958
Addie Darling, 1958–1960
June Ciampa, 1961–1962 and 1964–1965
Teddie Darling, 1962–1964
Sherry Carden, 1965–1966
Valerie Brown, 1966–1969
Selita Sue Smith, 1969–1973
Linda Hughes, 1973–1976
Kathy Burkle, 1976–1979
Susan Fron, 1979–1982
Sally Batina, 1982–1983
Valerie Ludwick, 1983–1987
Candice Nagle, 1987–1988
Dawn Beck, 1988–1989
Kim Ratcliffe, 1989–1990
Holly Fehrman, 1990–1994
Alisha Bane, 1994–1995
Dawn Vardaman, 1995–1996
Ann Loppnow, 1996–2000
Abby Moore, 2000–2001
Erin Ansfield, 2001–2002
Robyn Andrews, 2002–2003
Christy Jayne Stallings, 2003–2006
Meghan Lamontagne, 2006–2007
Tierney Brown, Spring 2008
MerrieBeth Cox, 2008–

Girls in Black Through History

June Ciampa (International Twirler), 1962–1963
Linda Hughes, 1971–1973
Pam Moschini, 1973–1974
Lisa Ross, 1974–1979
Susie Lilovich, 1979–1982
Janet Lowery, 1982–1985
Kim Ratcliffe, 1986–1989
Kelly Ratcliffe, 1989–1990
Angie Sword, 1990–1991
Alisha Bane, 1991–1994
Dawn Vardaman, 1994–1995
Cherri Reichard, 1995–1996
Karen Asadourian, 1996–1998
Nicole Ferree, 1998–2001
Robyn Andrews, 2001–2002
Krista Woodward, 2002–2004
Tierney Brown, 2004–2008
Erin Powell, 2008–2009
Meg Merdian, 2009–2012

Silver Twins Through History

Karon and Sharon Roeske, 1960–1963
Susan Ragsdale and Lana Barminski, 1963–1964
Janice and Jean Kelley, 1964
Judith and Jane Sorensen, 1964–1966
Janet Carlson and Karen Drotleff, 1966–1967
Janet and Joyce Carlson, 1967–1971
Sharon and Cheryl Fenzau, 1970–1973
Candi and Randi Brough, 1971–1975
Claudia and Stephanie Banvard, 1973–1974
Susan Johnson and Cyndy Love, 1976–1979
Linda and Sharon McCaffrey, 1977–1979
Jane and Jean Gilbert, 1980–1984
Kimberly Crum and Dawn Beck, 1985–1986
Billi and Lani Barnes, 1986–1990
Lisa and Renee Rhodes, 1990–1991
Robyn Beck and Dawn Vardaman, 1992–1993

Silver Twins Kimberly Crum and Dawn Beck

Ann Burman and Kelly Beyer, 1993–1994
Erin Griffin and Alisha Stenger, 1995–1997
Erin Buescher and Wendy King, 1998–2000
Krista Woodward and Kim Benson, 2001–2002
Tracey Johnson and Julie Thompson, 2003–2004
Megan and Morgan VonDielingen, 2004–2007
Sara and Chellie Zou, 2008–2012

CHAPTER SIX

IT'S GOT THE BEAT

World's Largest Drum

Previous page: The "World's Largest Drum" was the first thing fans saw at the 2010 Macy's Thanksgiving Day Parade, as it twirled on top of the big red star on the street.

This cartoon appeared in the *Indianapolis News* during the Al Wright era. Indiana University and others tried to steal the drum several times.

"I think it's the greatest tradition we have at Purdue."

—Director of Purdue University Bands Jay Gephart

You can't have a band without a bass drum. It strikes the beat of the music. It's a thump you hear with your ears and feel reverberating through your body. It's the heart of the band, pounding rhythmically to the tempo of the music. It keeps all the other elements of the band in line, on time.

If the bass drum is the heart of the band, then the big bass drum—the "World's Largest Drum"—at Purdue University is the heart and soul of the "All-American" Marching Band.

It is the oldest member of the band, dating back to 1921. There are band traditions such as the Block "P" formation that predate the drum, but new people continue those traditions each year.

The drum alone returns to campus every fall. Sure, someone has to hit it with baseball bat-sized beaters, but the drum makes an impression all its own, before its deep bass voice booms through a football stadium. It's a visual impression. People see the drum, and they know Purdue is in town.

More than any other tradition, the "World's Largest Drum" represents Purdue Bands. It has been featured all over the country. Former President Harry Truman has signed it. Neil Armstrong, the first man on the moon, has pounded it.

Out of commission from time to time suffering from the football-sounding injury of a cracked head, occasionally stolen, and at least once dropped, the drum has spanned Purdue history and countless memories.

It was the brainchild of Purdue's first Director of Bands Paul Spotts Emrick. Emrick was an innovator, an electrical engineer by profession, and a musician by avocation. Within fifteen years after he started directing at Purdue, he had already instituted band traditions that are still carried out today, not only in West Lafayette, but across the country.

In the era shortly after World War I, when he was looking for still more ideas to make his band stand out from the rest, he hit upon the idea of a big drum.

The idea was not completely original to Emrick. There were big drums in some college bands just before and after World War I. They had a diameter of approximately four feet, and people were constantly trying to make them bigger.

In the late nineteenth century, Emrick's father, Levi, raised money to purchase a large bass drum for the Rochester Citizens Band. However, it was nowhere near what Emrick contemplated for Purdue.

Exactly when the idea of a huge bass drum hit Emrick isn't known. Some band members claimed he had the idea on his mind as early as 1914. It is known that Emrick talked over his thoughts with a close friend, Harry Goldsberry, of Dayton, Indiana, at the close of World War I. The two decided it would be an excellent idea, and they considered the details of making a drum that was larger than any in use.

Probably in late 1920 or early 1921, Emrick took the idea to U. G. Leedy, president of the Indianapolis Leedy Manufacturing Company. The company manufactured drums, and the employees there immediately saw the public relations and advertising benefits in building a drum the size Emrick had in mind.

According to various newspaper accounts printed since, Emrick was in the dark about the maximum size of his proposed drum. "Just how large a drum is it possible to make?" he asked. Leedy answered, "You can make a drum as large as there are skins available to make the heads."

That was the major hurdle in big bass drums. The main

element limiting the size was that the heads were made of single animal skins. It was not easy to find animals that were big enough, and two animals were needed, one for each side.

Emrick left the size of the drum open during his early discussions. However, he did leave Leedy with instructions that Purdue was interested in as big a bass drum as could be made, and he was to be contacted if appropriate heads could be found.

On March 22, 1921, Leedy sent Emrick a letter stating the company had "been giving considerable thought to the special bass drum proposition and believe we have devised a practical means of making such an instrument, providing we can find fiber of sufficient size for the shell."

However, during subsequent letters written in 1921, company officials questioned some details of the plan.

In a letter to Emrick dated June 1, 1921, Leedy wrote that one hide had been found big enough for a seven-foot diameter drum, and they were searching for another.

As an addendum, he added, "We have wondered if you have ever considered the matter of transportation for the big bass drum. You would have no end of trouble getting it in and out of trains as the doors are neither seven feet high, nor, we believe, seven feet wide. We would like to hear from you as to what your intentions are in this respect."

Emrick was out of town when the letter arrived from Leedy, but on June 14 he returned to West Lafayette and immediately responded, indicating this was a factor he had not considered.

"I am of the opinion it should be made of such size as would slip in a baggage car door as I would want to take it with us quite often," he wrote. "I will investigate baggage car door sizes at once, and you will hear from me in the next day or so regarding size."

"World's Largest Drum" on the football field during its first year, 1921.

Two days later Leedy responded with the letter that most certainly assured that Purdue would complete this project and would find a baggage car big enough for its drum, rather than building a drum small enough for a baggage car.

In a letter dated June 16, 1921, Leedy said the company had found the second hide needed for a seven-foot diameter head, and added he hoped Emrick would send him the maximum dimensions of the drum quickly.

Leedy wanted the publicity value of building the "World's Largest Drum" and wasn't interested in making anything smaller. His company had already invested considerable time in planning a drum to fit the hides that had been found.

He gave Emrick a push by telling him that he was not the only band director interested in having a big bass drum.

Leedy wrote:

Indiana University is interested in a large bass drum as is the American Legion of this city. Both have applied to us to make them the largest bass drum in the world. We have postponed a definite reply to both of these parties until we find out what success we have with your instrument.

We brought up the question of transportation difficulties with both these parties, and their answer was that they didn't care anything about this possible inconvenience, and that if the instrument would not go on a railway car, they would transport it on a truck.

We are not sure that we shall want to make any more monster instruments like this, but the information will apprise you of the fact that other organizations have similar ideas to yours in mind, and if you see fit to let this fact influence your decision, we will be guided accordingly.

Right: A *Chicago Tribune* cartoon from 1931 pokes fun at how complicated it was to take the "World's Largest Drum" on the road.

Emrick found a railroad baggage car that could carry the drum, and even if he had not been able to find one, probably he would have gone ahead with the biggest drum possible before he would let Indiana University or anyone else build one larger than his.

One potential disaster was averted in time. When they began work on the "monster" drum, it was in a Leedy Manufacturing Company storeroom that had an exit too small to get the drum out once it was completed. When they caught the mistake, they changed the construction location and went back to work.

According to an *Indianapolis Star* account written by Olive Inez Dowling in 1943 (when many of the people who built the drum were still alive), as soon as the instrument was completed, everyone wanted to test it out and hear how it sounded.

"A large drum stick was made for the testing," she wrote. "It was [summer] and windows were open in the houses thereabout, and [there was] washing flapping gently on the lines. When the big drum was tested out, the volume was so deep that the good housewives thought it was thunder and rushed to take their clothes from the lines."

At Notre Dame they could "shake down the thunder from the sky," as the Fighting Irish song says. But at Purdue, with this new drum, the band would be able to make thunder of its own.

The drum appears at one of its first away games in 1921 versus the University of Chicago. Fans were so taken with the drum that they wanted one also.

It was a thunderous entrance to the world for the drum, which was something to behold. It weighed more than five hundred pounds, was somewhere in the area of three and a half feet wide and had a diameter of more than seven feet. It contained a metal underlay, and it was made of a five-ply laminated wood shell with extra-large maple counter hoops—the devices that hold the skin to the shell. Forty-eight tension rods were used. The circumference was about twenty-two feet.

At first, a small carriage was made for the drum. It used bicycle tires, but when the tires got stuck in the groove of streetcar tracks during an early parade, they decided a better system was needed, something with larger automobile tires. They selected a Ford chassis with Ford wheel mountings.

Leedy was as excited about the drum as Emrick, so when it came time to present it to the University, he invited news photographers. In addition to the still pictures taken that day, moving pictures were shot and were played at the Circle Theater in Indianapolis the week of August 14, 1921.

The only thing the cameras did not record was the exchange of money. The drum cost about $800, and that amount of money was hard to come by in 1921. There was at least one point when Leedy must have wondered if he ever would be paid.

HOW BIG IS BIG?

It was so big that the manufacturer had to halt fabrication when it realized that the door of the facility was too small to fit the drum through upon completion.

It was so big that at some schools the drum had to be hoisted overtop the stadium seats and carried down to the field as the stadium entrance was not large enough.

It was so big that a special call had to go out to find steer hides big enough to fit the head. Alumni would send pictures of prospective enormous bulls to the band director for consideration (later, the animal skin was replaced with Mylar).

"More than once the big bass drum and I almost collided," said former Purdue Golden Girl Susan Fron, who graduated in 1982. "And believe me, the drum would have won!"

To raise money, the band held a "Big Drum Benefit Concert" and received $489.95 in ticket sales with expenses totaling $54.95 for various printing costs—advertisements and programs.

The following additional donations were made from Lafayette businesses and organizations: Peerless Wire Company, $15; *Lafayette Journal and Courier*, $10; Brown Rubber Company, $10; American Legion Post 11, $10; Reamer Club, $10; Elks Club, $5; and Schwab Safe Company, $5.

That brought the total amount raised to $500 after expenses. The Lafayette Elks Club donated an additional $300.

The drum was in use before it was formally accepted by Purdue and taken to West Lafayette. The first place the drum went was to the Indiana Statehouse in Indianapolis, where it was put on display and received considerable attention.

According to newspaper accounts, it was then taken to the Indiana State Fair, where it was used during a week-long engagement. The Purdue band was at the State Fair in 1921 from September 5–10.

It was a real showstopper. From the first moment when the drum appeared, all eyes were riveted on its massive frame. However, problems quickly developed.

On March 18, 1922, Emrick sent a letter to Leedy beginning with the announcement that he was sending a picture of the drum "with my compliments." It also might have been sent to graphically point out problems.

"Due to contractions of the heads, the flesh hoops of the Big Drum have turned up on the edge," Emrick wrote. "I want to have the straining mechanism of this drum entirely rebuilt as it is too light and want also to make more clearance to allow for loosening of the heads to prevent distorting the flesh hoops. I do not want this drum to be a failure, but must acknowledge we did not take into account sufficiently the enormous expansion and contraction of such large heads."

The repairs were made.

The size of the drum always presented challenges. Lawrence Condrey, a band member who graduated in 1932, wrote in a band remembrance, "On the occasion of a trip to the University of Michigan, the drum was too big to go through the entrances to the stadium field. Hoisting it up to the top of the stadium wall and carrying it down over the seats to the field where it joined its carriage solved the problem."

In the winter of 1937, Emrick decided to have the drum rebuilt. On February 6, 1937, he wrote the Leedy Manufacturing Company, which had moved to Elkhart, concerning the cost of various repairs, including new heads. George W. Way, Leedy sales manager, responded with various prices. "Believe me, this is a very special price," he said. "We are as proud of the big drum as you are and would like to see it in the very best condition."

The company had heads big enough for the drum, indicating they had prepared for the needs of what they called the "monster." It went in for refurbishing in April. At that time the gold spackle and gold diamonds that are still featured were added. According to many reports, the drum also grew several inches in the rebuilding.

Band members load the drum into a pickup truck, its main form of transportation throughout its entire life, pictured here in 1954.

It was also in April of that year that Emrick came upon the idea of putting the big drum on the back of a pickup truck—"motorizing it," he said, for performances.

On April 3, 1937, he wrote to H. H. Horner of the Horner Motor Company in Lafayette. "We believe a Chevrolet Commercial pick-up truck would be suitable for this purpose," he said. "Will you kindly take this matter up with the Chevrolet Company to see if they will cooperate with us to the extent of giving us an exceedingly low price for this truck. Of course, they may placard it for advertising purposes in a proper manner."

He indicated he would like to use the drum in the upcoming Kentucky Derby Festival Parade, where the band had taken first place the two previous years.

On April 22, a Leedy Company spokesman wrote to Emrick, told him the drum was ready, and suggested he send the "Chevy up to get it. The band paid $538 for the truck.

The cost of refurbishing the drum was $292.04. That did not include a charge of $19.20 that Emrick did not pay, for a cover he sent back. It didn't fit.

"You may cancel this as the cover should have been tried on the drum before it was sent out," he said, matter of factly.

Problems soon returned. During the 1940 football season, the heads cracked while in use due to rapid temperature changes. In 1942 there was talk that the drum would be repaired, but there were much more important concerns during those war years. The drum was put on hold, and it was a hold that lasted many years.

A 1950 newspaper article stated the drum had been out of use for almost a decade and was therefore "probably unfamiliar to many students."

It was repaired for the 1950 football season but soon fell into disrepair again. When Al Wright arrived on campus in the summer of 1954, replacing Emrick, he found the drum out of commission.

Wright took the campus by storm, providing a new look to the band that first year and introducing the Golden Girl. But before he did either of those, he worked on the drum.

On September 8, 1954, he shipped the drum off to Leedy for new heads. "This will be the first time the drum has been used in several years," Wright said in a letter to the Purdue News Service. "We plan to use the big drum as sort of a symbol or trademark of Purdue Bands."

And that's what it became—a symbol of the band and the University. Wright would never again allow the drum to sit for any extended period of time in storage while waiting for repairs. When it needed repairs, people sometimes worked to the last minute to get it into shape.

In fact, when he first arrived on campus, Wright no sooner sent the drum off to get new heads than he wrote to the Agricultural Alumni Association asking that its members be on the lookout for steers big enough to provide hides for the drum.

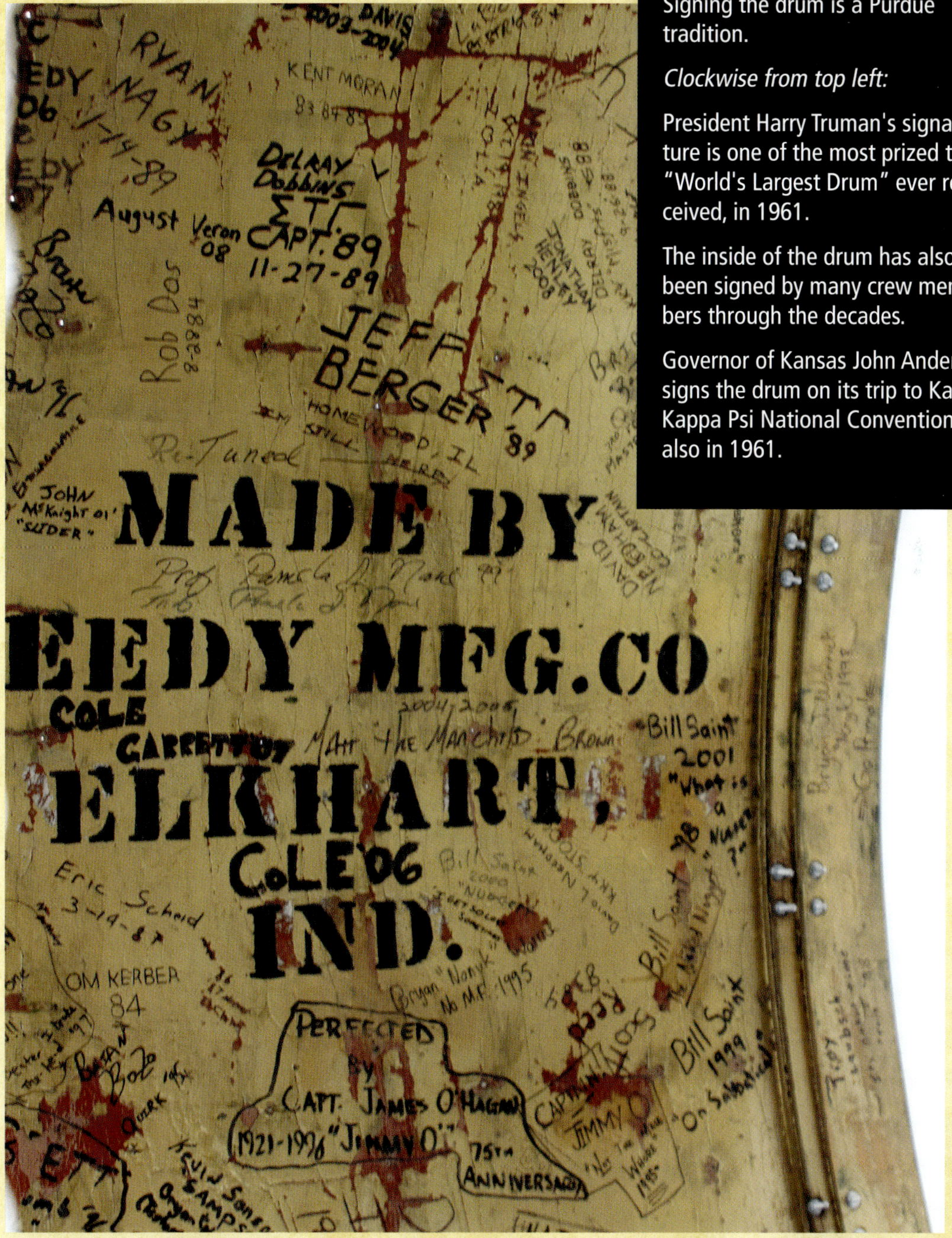

Sign here please...

Signing the drum is a Purdue tradition.

Clockwise from top left:

President Harry Truman's signature is one of the most prized the "World's Largest Drum" ever received, in 1961.

The inside of the drum has also been signed by many crew members through the decades.

Governor of Kansas John Anderson signs the drum on its trip to Kappa Kappa Psi National Convention, also in 1961.

Happy Birthday, "World's Largest Drum"

When the drum turned eighty in 2001, this big milestone required a big cake to match the occasion *(above)*. That year the "World's Largest Drum" participated in the Rose Bowl *(bottom right)* and the only surviving member of its original crew, Marc Gilbert, was honored at Homecoming *(top right)*.

A picture of the drum in the back of the Chevrolet pickup soon appeared in an Agricultural Alumni Association publication. "Here's an idea for a project for Ag Alumni," the caption read. "Let's have a big bull on hand to replace this drum head when the durned thing busts again."

Wright did get letters from alumni who had seen appropriately sized bulls. Some even sent photographs.

During the next several years, the drum continued to make appearances on the back of the Chevrolet. In 1957 the engineers in the band rigged up a platform so the drum revolved slowly in the bed of the truck.

The problem of broken heads continued to plague Wright. Ranchers were breeding a smaller steer than they had in 1921 when the drum was built to fit the biggest hides they could find. Wright knew if a head broke—and sooner or later it always did—there would be a problem finding a replacement.

So, on September 19, 1960, he sent a letter that would change the history of the drum. It was addressed to the DuPont research laboratory in Wilmington, Delaware, and said, "Here at Purdue University we have a giant bass drum. We have some difficulty in obtaining proper calf-skin drum heads for this instrument. I am wondering if your Mylar, which I understand is the material from which plastic drum heads are made, is available in sufficient width for use on this drum."

The plastic was not available in sufficient widths for the drum, but there were Purdue alumni who worked for DuPont, and they took a personal interest. One of them went in at night on his own time to run off sheets of the material large enough to be made into a head.

By 1963 Remo, Inc., of North Hollywood, California, was making plastic heads for the drum from the Mylar purchased from DuPont. Correspondence between the band department and the company were quite regular from that point on, especially annually in early September before the first home football game and early May before the Indianapolis 500 when an ordered head had not arrived.

In 1922, one year after the Purdue drum had premiered, the University of Chicago commissioned its own big drum. It was first used in 1922 in a game against Princeton University. The drum was named "Big Bertha" for the German World War I "Big Bertha" howitzer. There was a long-running controversy over whether Purdue or Chicago did, indeed, have the world's largest drum.

In 1939 the University of Chicago dropped its football program, and the drum was stored beneath the stands at Stagg Field. During World War II, part of the nuclear bomb development research for the Manhattan Project took place under the stands, and the drum became radioactively contaminated.

In 1955 a University of Texas alumnus and former band member bought "Big Bertha" for $1, had it decontaminated, and it has been used by the Longhorn band ever since.

By 1961 the Purdue "World's Largest Drum" versus "Big Bertha" controversy had been brewing for nearly forty years. The time had come to settle the question once and for all, at least as far as a group of band members at Purdue were concerned.

Purdue University members of Kappa Kappa Psi, the band honorary fraternity, challenged the members of Kappa Kappa Psi at Texas to bring their drum to the fraternity's 1961 convention in Wichita, Kansas. There, the drums would be placed side by side and a winner declared.

The Purdue band members found an old drum head and wrote a challenge on it to the Texas drummers. "Bring your drum to Wichita," the Purdue group said. "We'll bring ours and we'll measure them side by side."

Furthermore, the Purdue band group, in a burst of energy that can only come from college students with some free

The Drum Gets a Facelift

In 1937, Emrick sent the "World's Largest Drum" back to the Leedy Company for a facelift. Previously the maple-shelled drum had sported a natural wood finish, but it came out this time with the gold sparkle and gold diamonds that are still seen on the drum today. According to many reports, the drum grew several inches in the rebuilding. The total cost of the refurbishing was $292.04.

George Foster (left) and Earl Jenkins (right) get the "World's Largest Drum" ready to send in for repairs in September 1954.

Coldest Marching Day in Purdue History?

Denver was one of several cities where the "All-American" Marching Band gave a parade on its way to the 1967 Rose Bowl. The temperature in the Mile High City was so cold it caused one of the "World's Largest Drum" heads to rupture. The head was replaced before the Rose Bowl parade and game, but there was no time to paint "Purdue" on it, so the drum crew had to be careful to keep its "good" side toward the camera.

Crew members pushed the drum through every major city on a trip from West Lafayette to Wichita, Kansas, to have a showdown with the Texas drum. Texas, however, was a no-show.

time on their hands, challenged the Texas band members to push their drum through every big city en route to Wichita, and Purdue students would do the same thing coming from West Lafayette.

The University of Texas Kappa Kappa Psi members eagerly accepted the challenge, telling the Purdue band members to get out the paint remover to erase "World's Largest Drum" from their drum head.

Roy Johnson, class of 1960 and a clarinet player, went on that trip, and he remembers little concern on the part the band department in giving the drum to a bunch of guys to push halfway through the Midwest. "As long as we took the proper precautions, the University didn't seem too concerned," Johnson said.

Maybe, but let the official record read that Wright asked the University to take out a $6,000 "all risk" insurance policy on the drum for the period it would be gone—August 14 to September 2.

The fourteen band members in the group set out from West Lafayette on Monday, August 14, and hit Indianapolis, the first big city they planned to push the drum through, at 2 p.m. By the time the mayor finished a ceremony with the drum at Monument Circle, it was 4 p.m. and the start of rush hour. Then, it started to rain.

It took more than an hour to push the drum out of Indianapolis that afternoon, and the group was beginning to wonder if their challenge was such a great idea.

Out of town at last, they loaded the drum on their Chevrolet pickup truck and drove toward St. Louis. They did not reach St. Louis until 2 a.m. the next day. By the time they got settled in their hotel rooms, it was 3 a.m.

At 8:30 the next morning, they were at it again, pushing their drum through St. Louis. In each big city they had public officials and other well-known people autograph the drumhead.

The students made arrangements for warehousing the drum overnight in every city where they slept, and they picked the safest places they could find. When they stopped for the night, the drum was parked in police garages.

The morning after they pushed through St. Louis, the group got up and had breakfast in Kansas City, Missouri. As they ate, several Missouri State Police officers came over to their table.

What was the problem? Pushing a giant drum without a license? Reckless drumming?

No. The police had been searching all over trying to locate the group to escort them through town. The seven-foot drum parked in a pickup truck outside the restaurant had been a dead giveaway.

After a long push through Kansas City, the drum was loaded on the truck at the city limits. They no sooner got the instrument loaded than the television crews arrived, so down came the drum, and they pushed it around some more.

On the fourth day they were pushing the drum through Topeka, Kansas, having already received the signatures of several mayors and the governor of the state. They had been named honorary citizens of Kansas City and received the key to the city. That's when they got the biggest autograph of the trip.

Lyle Cameron, Purdue class of 1948, was president of the Purdue Club of Kansas City, and he was helping the group with its project. One of the students asked Cameron if they were near former President Harry Truman's house, and Cameron said, yes, it was just down the road.

"Can we ask him to autograph the drum?" a student asked.

You don't get anywhere without asking, and even though the request sounded impossible, the students had asked the right person. Cameron knew Truman's private secretary. He placed a call, and it was arranged.

They drove 150 miles in the pouring rain to Independence, Missouri. It was still raining when they arrived, but Truman came outside his house to see the drum anyway. A large crowd of people gathered on the street as two secret service agents lifted Truman onto the bed of the truck so he could sign the head.

Many of the band members were wearing senior cords—corduroy pants—painted with fraternity and other college symbols and sayings, a popular tradition in the 1950s and early 1960s.

The drum is never relegated to the sidelines, playing a specific role in every show the bandperforms, pictured here in 2009.

"Why did you get your pants all cluttered up with things like that?" Truman asked them.

He signed the drum, enjoyed the story about how the Purdue group would prove once and for all that their drum was the biggest, and joked with everyone around him.

"Don't any of you guys ever get haircuts?" he asked, laughing.

When they finally reached Wichita, they were flat broke. There were nineteen students, three trucks, and four automobiles in the "parade," and all the expenses had come out of their own pockets, but finally they would be able to prove their drum was bigger than the Texas drum. They wheeled their charge to the convention site, ready for the face-to-face, head-to-head test. The only problem was, the Texas drum never showed up. The students from Texas didn't bring their drum.

There was nothing to do but declare that Purdue owned the "World's Largest Drum" and return home.

That trip went without mishap for the drum, but not all journeys went so well. In May of 1976, the drum was being carried on the back of a pickup truck down I-65 for its annual appearance at the Indianapolis 500.

Everything was going smoothly until the truck hit a bump, the kind of bump that appears in Indiana roads after a winter of freezing and thawing. The truck bounced and the drum flew into the air, right off the back of the truck.

It broke loose from the chains that held it down, and it landed on the interstate. As the pickup barreled down the highway, the drum rolled along behind. It finally did stop, which was good, but the bad part was, it was stopped by an eighteen-wheeler. In addition to other damage, the drum suffered a broken rim.

When the band arrived in Indianapolis, they patched the drum as best they could, to the point where they could play it on one side. On the other side, the drum crew members just pretended to strike the big head.

Drum thieves also caused havoc over the years.

A big drum is a natural target for big pranksters, and, Purdue's big bass drum has been stolen occasionally. A college prank has always been the motive behind the theft, and irreparable damage has never been done.

"There have been times when it was missing, and the police would call and say, 'It's been seen going north,'" Wright said. "Then I tell them it's going to South Bend. If it's headed south, it's headed for Bloomington. All the police have to do is wait for them on the outskirts of town."

One year it disappeared and turned up on a Purdue golf course. Rain damaged the heads, and it was out of commission for a year. Another time it was successfully drum-napped to Bloomington, where it was proudly paraded around during Indiana University Homecoming festivities.

It was returned when it was spotted and identified. "The Purdue band recognized it right away as theirs," an Indiana University alumnus quipped.

Every time it is stolen, the incident brings nationwide publicity to the drum. That fact caused Wright to once state, "If nobody stole it once every ten years or so, I'd steal it myself."

One of the most intriguing drum-naps occurred on October 26, 1979, the night before a Purdue versus Northwestern football game at Ross-Ade Stadium. The band performed at Homecoming the next day minus the big bass drum. On Monday, October 29, it was publicly announced that the drum had been taken.

A drum ransom note was all the band members had found in the Armory—where it was stored—on Saturday morning. The note said: "PU—We've got it. You want it. What's it worth to you? Reply in campus newspaper—NU."

Purdue police revealed that the Armory had been open late Friday night because of boxing matches, and there were skid marks leading to the door where the drum must have been taken out. But how could the perpetrators remove the drum without being seen?

Reports came in that the drum had been seen rolling around campus late Friday night, but nothing could be verified.

It was finally found on Tuesday, October 30, located in an Armory balcony behind an air conditioner, an area accessible only by a ladder. The question of how the perpetrators hoisted the drum up there was quickly replaced by another problem.

Drum Tricks

The size of the "World's Largest Drum" required some athleticism to merely beat it. In the years following the new millennium, aerial tricks became common, including leaping off the drum.

Neil Armstrong, a former Purdue "All-American" Marching Band member, hits the "World's Largest Drum" during an Astronaut Reunion in 1999.

How would the band members get it back down?

It required a crane.

On January 1, 2001, the day Purdue played the University of Washington in the Rose Bowl, the big bass drum found itself featured on the cover of the *Los Angeles Times* sport pages. The drum was interviewed by columnist Bill Plaschke.

"Will we notice you today?" Plaschke asked the drum.

"You'll notice little else," the big bass drum said. "I'll spin, I'll shake. I'll sprint downfield . . ."

"Do you have any enemies?" Plaschke asked.

The drum replied, "Put it this way, in Columbus I am pelted with buckeyes. In Ann Arbor I am hit with snowballs. At the Alamo Dome, some joker nailed me with frozen tortillas."

"Do the students [in the band] get paid well?" Plaschke continued.

"They are paid nothing," the drum said. "Purdue doesn't even have a music major. The kids usually work at least ten hours a week, usually more, for a couple of hours of band credit . . . . But you know what they say? They say 'Instead of just attending Purdue, we feel like we are Purdue.'"

Members of the "All-American" Marching Band still feel like they are Purdue. They always will. And they will always have the "World's Biggest Drum" to beat. They take special pride in it during the last home football game of the season when senior band members are introduced and take turns beating the drum.

"We're very careful with this drum," Director of Bands Jay Gephart said. "Ludwig or someone could probably build us another one. But it could never replace this one. The construction is so special. Members of the drum crew over the years have signed it. It's been everywhere. When I travel people ask me if we still have that drum.

"It's our icon."

CHAPTER SEVEN

A CENTURY OF TRADITION

The Indianapolis 500

Previous page: Dinah Shore sings "Back Home Again in Indiana" with the band at the Indianapolis 500 in 1955.

In the spring of 1954, Al and Gladys Wright were celebrating. He had just received a letter naming him director of bands at Purdue University. He wasn't even positive what Purdue meant by "director." In Miami, Florida, where he taught high school, they used the word "conductor."

However, he had an idea what was going on. "By being director of bands, that meant no one else in the department could tell me what to do," Wright said. "I only had to report to the vice president."

That sounded wonderful to Wright.

He and Gladys had only been married nine months, and when she came home that evening she found her husband holding the job offer letter from the University. The Purdue position paid $7,200 a year, $3,200 more than his job in the high school. Dinner and movie served as the couple's celebration for the new opportunity.

When the Wrights entered the theater a newsreel was playing featuring the upcoming Indianapolis 500. As Wright walked down the dark aisle, he looked up at the huge screen in front of him and there, marching toward him, was the Purdue "All-American" Marching Band captured by a cameraman standing on the famed oval track. The band members filled the screen as they moved toward the camera, playing as they marched.

It was Wright's first experience standing in front of the band, and it would be his place for the next twenty-seven years. It also was the first time he realized the magnitude of the job he was undertaking. Wright, himself, would go on to become an institution and a leader at the Indianapolis Motor Speedway until his retirement in 1981.

The Purdue "All-American" March Band is rich with longstanding traditions, from the "World's Largest Drum," to the Block "P" formation, to the Golden Girl and Silver Twins. Tradition has been part of the band from the very beginning.

The band matches perfectly with one of the most tradition-filled events and festivals in the world—the Indianapolis 500 Mile Race.

Doug Boles, director of public relations for the Indianapolis Motor Speedway, said the bond between Purdue and the race runs deep.

"Purdue is a leader in technology, engineering, and the Indianapolis Motor Speedway is a leader in implementing technology, putting it to the test on our track," he said. "Both Purdue and the Indianapolis Motor Speedway have contributed significantly to our nation's technology innovation."

In terms of the last two hours before the race begins and the pageantry surrounding the festivities, the Purdue "All-American" Marching Band is an important tradition, he said.

"The band playing and the drum being driven around the track—families make a tradition out of getting to the race to see the drum and the band," Boyle continued. "Purdue and the Motor Speedway are all about tradition and Indiana."

The year 2011 is not only the band's 125th anniversary; it marks the 100th Indianapolis 500 Mile Race.

"We're hoping one hundred years from now we'll still be talking about the Purdue, Motor Speedway relationship," Boyle said.

The first race at the Indianapolis Motor Speedway took place on May 30, 1911, when the track was only two years old. In 1911 the Purdue band was already celebrating its 25th anniversary and was a widely known and loved musical organization throughout the state.

The band entertains fans at the 1946–1947 Indianapolis 500. The Speedway at that time was comprised entirely of brick.

Clockwise from top left: "World's Largest Drum" on a rotating platform in the 1950s; Al Wright conducting in the 1950s; playing "Taps" at the Speedway, 1955–1956.

With Paul Spotts Emrick as director, the band performed in parades and events in Indiana and was gaining an increasing popularity in Indianapolis.

In June of 1919, the band was picked to lead a victory parade in Indianapolis celebrating the end of World War I. Nearly 200,000 people lined the streets. May of 1919 was also the year that the Purdue band made its first appearance at the Indianapolis Motor Speedway. It is a tradition that has continued ever since.

Legendary drivers such as Peter DePaolo, Louis Meyer, Wilbur Shaw, A. J. Foyt, Mario Andretti, Al Unser, Bobby Unser, and Rick Mears have come and gone, but the Purdue band marches on.

It was Emrick who formed the initial relationship with the Motor Speedway and its owners at that time—Carl G. Fisher, James A. Allison, Arthur C. Newby, and Frank H. Wheeler.

In 1917 and 1918, racing stopped at the Motor Speedway because of World War I, as it would again in the early 1940s during World War II. The Memorial Day running of the "500" in May of 1919, coupled with the June Victory Parade in Indianapolis, must have seemed like one big celebration and the Purdue band a natural partner.

According to Indianapolis Motor Speedway historian Donald Davidson, it was probably in 1919 when race officials decided to add more pageantry to the event. They came up with a unique idea. They invited anyone who could play an instrument to come to the Motor Speedway and perform as part of a mass band before the race. In return, the musicians entered the venue for free.

As a large and highly organized unit, the Purdue "All-American" Marching Band played a prominent role. A 1922 photograph of the mass band shows men dressed in many different uniforms standing on the track, instruments in hand. The "World's Largest Drum" towers behind them.

Paul Spotts Emrick directs in the 1940s.

In the twenty-first century, the Purdue "All-American" Marching Band is the official band of the Indianapolis 500 and performs much of the music for the opening ceremonies.

One of the greatest traditions uniting the Purdue band and the Indianapolis 500 is the song "Indiana," better known as "Back Home Again in Indiana":

Back home again in Indiana
And it seems that I can see
The gleaming candlelight, still burning bright
Through the sycamores for me
The new mown hay sends all its fragrance
Through the fields I used to roam
When I dream about the moonlight on the Wabash
And I long for my Indiana home.

View from the grandstands, 1950.

The song was published in January of 1917 and was written by James Hanley, who was born in Indiana, and Ballard MacDonald, who had no connection to the state. It was immediately popular and became a jazz standard. It also borrowed heavily from another piece that in 1913 had been designated the official song of the state, "On the Banks of the Wabash, Far Away." It was written by another Hoosier-born songwriter, Paul Dresser. Published in 1897, the song also met with great success:

Oh, the moonlight's fair tonight along the Wabash
From the fields there comes the breath of new
mown hay
Through the sycamores the candle lights are gleaming
On the banks of the Wabash, far away.

While Dresser's song was first and had been designated the official song of Indiana, its two choruses are melancholy. They focus on longing for a mother and a youthful sweetheart, both of whom have died.

The song's mood just did not seem appropriate for the start of what would eventually be known as "The Greatest Spectacle in Racing."

There are reports that "Indiana" was first performed by a trackside band in 1919 as Howdy Wilcox won that year's race. If so, it might have been played by the Purdue band.

When the Indianapolis 500 resumed after World War II in 1946, the song officially became part of the pre-race festivities. It was performed by James Melton, of the New York Metropolitan Opera. He sang the song over the public address system about forty-five minutes before the start of the race, accompanied by the Purdue "All-American" Marching Band.

It was so popular that the song became a tradition, and in 1948 it took over the slot that it still holds—played just prior to starting the racecar engines.

The Purdue band also plays "On the Banks of the Wabash, Far Away" during pre-race ceremonies, but the Motor Speedway gives "Indiana" the featured spot.

Among those who have performed the song with the Purdue band are Mel Tormé, Vic Damone, Dinah Shore, Ed Ames, Peter Marshall, Dennis Morgan, and Johnny Desmond. Jim Nabors has done it almost every year since 1972, though he did not realize he was starting a tradition when he first sang at the race.

In 1972 Nabors was a guest of hotel and casino owner Bill Harrah, and his plans were to just enjoy the race. However, track owner, Tony Hulman, Jr., talked to him and asked if he would like to "sing the song."

Nabors agreed, thinking Hulman meant the national anthem. Later, when Purdue "All-American" Marching Band Director Al Wright told him he would be performing "Indiana," Nabors was quite surprised. He knew the song but wasn't sure of all the words, so he wrote them on his hands before the performance.

Without any rehearsal, Nabors and the Purdue band performed "Indiana" for hundreds of thousands of onlookers gathered at the speedway and millions more watching on television and listening on the radio.

The song "God Bless America" is also featured before every race and has been performed by many famous signers, accompanied by the Purdue band. However, none of the singers is more widely known than Florence Henderson.

A native of Dale, Indiana, Henderson's career has spanned Broadway, movies, and television. She has performed at the race every year since 1995 (and occasionally prior to 1995).

"I enjoy the spontaneity, the excitement, the crowd, the race itself," Henderson said.

The only rehearsal with the Purdue band is a discussion right before the race, but she loves working with the Boilermakers.

"I have enjoyed it immensely," Henderson said. "The Purdue band is terrific."

A twirler jokes around with Jim Nabors, a track favorite for his rendition of "Back Home Again in Indiana," in the 1990s.

One of her most memorable moments at the track came while performing with former Director of Bands David Leppla.

"I loved working with Dave," she said. "One year they started the race car engines in the middle of the song by mistake. When the noise stopped, I was on pitch and we were perfectly together. Bravo to Dave and the Purdue band."

Leppla said the incident "rattled" him, and they kept together through eye contact.

"She is such a professional," he said. "She's been through lots of similar incidents. That's show business."

In 1950 the band made a movie appearance with Clark Gable. Gable and Barbara Stanwyck were stars of the MGM film *To Please a Lady*, in which Gable plays a racecar driver. The movie centers on the Indianapolis Motor Speedway and the 500 Mile Race.

In the movie, the band is shown marching out of the southwest turn before the race with the music of glocken-

Facing page: Florence Henderson, pictured here in the 1990s, always takes time to pose with the band members when she sings during the opening ceremonies.

spiels in the background. The band is also shown standing at attention as the cars are rolled to the starting line and later as the race begins.

In 1955 the band took its annual trip to the Motor Speedway and performed "Indiana" with the star of radio, television, and movies, Dinah Shore. Wright remembered looking up at her on a stand as he held up his baton, preparing the band to begin.

"Whenever you are ready, Miss Shore," Wright said.

"Oh no, maestro," she said. "It's whenever you are ready."

Her protocol was correct, and it showed the respect she had for the Purdue band.

It was Wright's first year at the Indianapolis 500, but he quickly made an impression with spectators at the Motor Speedway. In 1957 the race committee added a parade through downtown Indianapolis, and the "All-American" Marching Band took part, along with a number of high school bands. When the University's band was presented with a trophy for placing first in the parade marching band competition, Wright promptly sent it back.

"I told them my band was not in the parade for evaluation," Wright said. "We were marching for entertainment. There were a lot of good high school bands in the parade, but to put a high school band up against the Purdue band in competition wasn't fair. The people from the 500 got back with me and said, 'Okay, you're unhappy. We don't know what we're doing with this. Why don't you come down and run it for us.'"

So he did. He took his years of experience from the Orange Bowl Festival when he was a high school band conductor in Miami and put them to use in Indianapolis. From 1959 until his retirement from Purdue, Wright served in various capacities with the Indianapolis 500 Festival Committee, including a continuous run as chairman of the band selection committee.

Since 1957 the Purdue "All-American" Marching Band has remained the first and main musical group in the parade.

At the time of the race and festivities, the regular academic year has ended and students are scattered across the country and the world in their home communities for the summer. Participation in the event is therefore voluntary with many band members traveling great distances at their own expense to take part in the weekend's exciting events.

The parade never fails to be a grueling one when a heavy, full-body wool uniform and Purdue's high-energy marching style is combined with Indiana summer heat and humidity, amplified by the hot asphalt of the downtown Indianapolis streets.

On race day, the band members reach the rally point at a nearby mall where they are met by their police escort, which leads the group to the racetrack. Once inside, there is a short rehearsal and warm-up before beginning their march around the track to the finish line, beginning in the third turn. They reach the pit area around 10:30 a.m., ready for the opening ceremony. In recent years as the start of the race has been pushed back, the band has performed for fans behind the Pagoda.

Band members have great memories of their role in the Indianapolis 500.

In 1969 the band was included in a Paul Newman movie about the race, entitled *Winning.*

"Listening to the crowd cheer the Purdue band was always the best!" said Dan Becker in a band remembrance. "And then there was that little thing about appearing in the movie *Winning* and realizing I could be recognized as marching in the front row of the Purdue band in a major Hollywood movie!"

Alumni Band marches down the Speedway track, celebrating ninety years in 2009.

Tracy Hine Bullion played trombone and graduated in 1985. In a remembrance, she wrote, "In1982 I had just finished my freshman year. I was in the front rank and we stopped right on the finish line on the bricks. All eight of us got chills from the history. When we went into the pits and we were playing, Jim Nabors walked by. Everyone was whispering and I, being the quiet person I was, yelled, 'HEY, GOMER!' Well we started playing another song, but he came up to me and we started dancing together right there in the pits. It was a blast! Of course I was looking really attractive in my uniform. We got done dancing, Mr. Nabors thanked me, and then a California radio station came up to interview me on what it felt like to dance with Jim Nabors and my reaction!!"

"I recall quite vividly the 1983 '500' when I had the chance to drive around the famous Indy oval," Mark Maisonneuve, a tuba player who graduated in 1984, wrote in his remembrance.

"I had broken my left foot jumping off the back wall at Slayter Center and had to deal with a cast for the [event]," he said. "I could not march, but I did manage to finagle my way onto the Big Bass Drum crew. Their job was to drive the drum all around the track in the back of a pickup truck. My job was to stand on the rear bumper and hold the drum. I realize now that the drum was far safer then we were as we went whizzing around the track, but at the time it was the coolest thing!"

Sally Batina was the Purdue Golden Girl in 1982 and 1983, and the Indianapolis 500 is one of her best memories.

"At my final performance at the Indianapolis 500 I had the opportunity to have my picture taken with Jim Nabors after he sang 'Back Home Again in Indiana,' and that picture appeared in one of the Indianapolis papers the next day," she said. "I also was invited to watch part of the race from the tower where I met Paul Newman. I was so starstruck that all I could say was 'Hello, Mr. Newman!' As I walked down the stairs of the tower, people were taking pictures like crazy. I felt like a star! For safety reasons, I had to have a police escort follow me back to the band buses. Talk about feeling like a celebrity!"

Dave Kantor has special memories of the race in 1987:

One of my favorite parts of the day was when the celebrities would get out of their cars after their parade lap around the track and mingle with the marching band members as we waited to perform the pre-race ceremonies. On this particular day, Chuck Yeager [the first person to fly a plane faster than the speed of sound] glanced towards me as I held my trombone and he hopped out of his pace car. He was headed straight for me! He stuck out his hand and said with a big smile, "So, you must

The band marches down Meridian Street in 2004 behind Drum Majors Danielle Donovan and Bob Shriner.

Clockwise from left: Goldusters featured at a Speedway performance in 2001; Golden Girl Addie Darling leads the band in 1959; Majorettes dance down the track in 1964.

play the trombone!" I replied, "I hear you fly airplanes!" We both got a big chuckle after we both stated the obvious. I then told him that I was a fellow aviator and had just graduated Purdue with a BS in Aviation Technology. I told him that I had about one thousand hours of flying time and was currently looking for a job with an airline. He said, "Fantastic! Good luck with your career in aviation!"

Two weeks later, I started reading Chuck Yeager's autobiography, Yeager, that I had received as a graduation gift. In one of the first chapters, I read that Chuck Yeager had played the trombone when he was in school! I couldn't believe it! If I had that moment in time back, I would have handed him my trombone, put my uniform hat on his head and let him play "Hail Purdue!" Regardless of an opportunity lost, it was one of my fondest Indianapolis 500 memories. I had a chance to meet the first person to break the sound barrier.

Ted Rich, who played baritone, graduated in 1991 and went on to become a car mechanic at the race for four years. His memories focus on a rainy, slippery Indianapolis 500 parade. "They did not get out all the shampoo from the checkered flag carpet, and a few of the Big Bass Drum Crew 'went down' in history that day," he wrote in a remembrance.

"My favorite memory of the Indy 500 is catching Steven Tyler's harmonica after he played/sang the "Star Spangled Banner" at the 2001 race," wrote former trumpet player David Hornthal in his remembrance. "Tyler, the lead singer of Aerosmith, was the solo vocalist for the national anthem that year. He was standing on a podium that was above the band. He started out with a harmonica solo and then started singing the anthem. When he started singing, he tossed his harmonica and it came right into the band. I looked up and it was coming towards me. I reach up to grab it, and it hit me in the palm and fell to the ground. Fortunately it stayed close and I was able to scoop up my fumble. I now own a piece of one of the worst national anthems in Indy 500 history—the one that ended, 'and the home of the Indianapolis 500.'"

Controversy surrounded Steven Tyler's rendition of the "Star Spangled Banner" in 2001.

Left: Band members begged actor Russell Crowe to pose with them, and he graciously obliged.

Right: Comedian Jay Leno directs the band in 1999.

The band performs during the 2009 Indianapolis 500 Festival Parade.

Tyler skipped the final words to the national anthem, "and the home of the brave," adding the alternate ending, for which he was widely criticized.

Memories from the Indianapolis Motor Speedway never seem to fade for members of the Purdue "All-American" Marching Band.

John Eckert, who graduated in 1956, can vividly remember performing at the race in 1953. He wrote about the experience in a remembrance to Purdue Bands.

That year (1953) "Paul Spotts Emrick stood with Met singer James Melton, raised his baton, and directed his last piece as the director of the Purdue University band," Eckert wrote. "The piece was, of course, 'Back Home Again in Indiana,' a fitting finale to [Emrick's] distinguished career. The last chords were quickly swallowed with applause, the excited cries of the crowd, and the sound of engines roaring to life."

Eckert remembers the steep bank of the first turn, marching in his wool uniform with the temperature in the low nineties, and sitting on the brick raceway on the main straightaway. He also remembers seeing actress Marie Wilson and other celebrities.

"One big thrill for me was I got to meet my childhood hero Roy Rogers," Eckert wrote. "Rogers was close to the band before we started to perform, and I went up to ask if I could take his photo. He agreed, provided he could take a movie of me."

At the age of seventy-four, Eckert still played the tuba in a classical orchestra in his hometown of Oregon, a British brass band in California, and a community band in Bryan, Ohio. "I live deep in a forest and practice on the back porch looking out at the trees," he said.

"Often, 'Back Home Again in Indiana' drifts through those woods . . ."

CHAPTER EIGHT

IMPROVISATIONS ON A THEME

Jazz, Concert bands, and Orchestra

Previous page: Purdue Jazz Band introduced a Valentine's Day "Evening of Romance" in the 1990s, which became an annual event. Soloist Alex Chiaghana performs here.

Below: Postcard from early 1900s depicts Purdue Orchestra in Fowler Hall.

President Ronald Reagan came to the Purdue University campus on April 9, 1987, to honor the school's engineering and technology programs.

He also took time to honor Purdue band members, who played for more than twenty thousand people assembled to greet Reagan at the University Airport and for more than ten thousand who waited for three hours to hear the president speak in Mackey Arena.

"Thank you, thank you all," Reagan said when he began his presentation in Mackey, after the band had finished playing "Ruffles and Flourishes" and "Hail to the Chief."

He then asked everyone to join him in wishing a happy 100th anniversary to Purdue University Bands, which had reached the milestone the year before.

"It isn't true that I was around for the first one," Reagan joked to loud approval from the crowd.

It was the first time that Purdue University Bands had performed for a current president of the United States, marking another great achievement for a musical organization that has now touched three centuries.

The title of the instrumental music department at Purdue is University Bands and Orchestras. More than eight hundred students take part in Purdue's seventeen bands and orchestras, providing an incredible array of opportunities in addition to the "All-American" Marching Band.

The different groups that have been part of the program over the years include: the "All-American" Marching Band; the Wind Ensemble; the Symphonic Band; the Concert Band; the Collegiate Band; the Varsity Band; the University Band; the Ceremonial Band; the Regimental Band; the Variety Band; the Purdue Jazz Band; the Lab Jazz Band; the Concert Jazz Band; the American Music Review; the American Music Repertory Ensemble; the Symphony Orchestra; the Philharmonic Orchestra; the Purdue Symphonette; the Purdue Ukulele Orchestra; the Strolling Strings; the Studio Orchestra; the Renaissance Ensemble; the Brass, Woodwind, Chamber, and Percussion Ensembles; the Gold and Black Sound; the Boiler Brass; the Boiler Box Band; and the Fanfare Trumpets.

For a university that does not have a school of music, the department is huge.

Director of Bands Jay Gephart said the goal is to meet the interests of a wide variety of students who come to Purdue with different musical backgrounds.

The program's expansion began with the arrival of Al Wright as director of bands in 1954.

"Al was great at trying new things," Gephart said. "He would try anything that gave the students an opportunity to perform and that helped promote the department."

In the early days, Paul Spotts Emrick traveled with his band around the state to perform, but Wright took a different approach. His bands performed on campus, and he invited nationally and internationally known guest conductors and musicians to perform with the group.

This tradition continues to this day with events such as the Purdue Band Showcase in the spring. Each year a nationally prominent composer comes to campus to interact with students for a week and conduct each of the concert bands.

"They talk about the history of the piece they've written and what inspired them," Gephart said. "It's an incredible opportunity for our students. I know from talking to people around the country that our students actually have more access to this kind of personal exposure to accomplished composers than students in most schools of music."

Opportunities to take part in different kinds of musical groups grew dramatically in the 1960s, about the same time male students at Purdue were no longer required to take one year of ROTC—a requirement that could be fulfilled by performing in the band.

"In the 1960s, the department as a whole exploded in numbers," Gephart said. This was due to the fact that women started performing in non-marching bands. "A lot of students who didn't want to be part of the marching band came into the program to pursue their areas of interest."

As the number of students grew, so did the quality of the band programs, and by the late 1960s, Wright took his Symphonic Band to perform at the American Bandmasters Association. It was the first time a Purdue instrumental ensemble played at a major national conference, and many more would follow.

One of the most popular band programs on campus was the Twilight Concert, which was held in late spring during the 1980s and continued until the early 2000s.

The special performance included four nights of concerts at Slayter Center, a series that traditionally ended with a rousing performance of the "1812 Overture." This song quickly became a student favorite because it allowed them to dance and splash in Slayter's reflecting pool.

Purdue has one of the most extensive concert band programs in the country, offering six different bands with membership based on musical ability and a varied approach to programming.

One of the most selective programs in Purdue Bands is the Wind Ensemble, which evolved from the Symphonic Band. It is directed by Gephart and includes the finest instrumentalists on campus.

Performances of the Wind Ensemble and its predecessors have featured nationally recognized guest soloists as well as solo performances by the Purdue Applied Music faculty. Its rich history includes performances under the baton of some of the world's finest conductors, ranging from John Philip Sousa to Arthur Fiedler, and from Karl King to Harry Begian. Recent soloists have included Patrick Sheridan, an internationally famous tuba virtuoso, and Rex Richardson, a former member of Dallas Brass and professor of trumpet at Virginia Commonwealth University.

Outdoor band concerts at Slayter Center date back to 1964 when the facility, donated by former Purdue tuba player Games Slayter and his wife Marie, was dedicated.

Guest composers who have worked with all the concert bands include Frank Ticheli, Timothy Mahr, David Holsinger, Robert Jager, David Gillingham, Philip Sparke, Roger Cichy, Ray Cramer, and Steven Bryant.

"Echoes of Indiana," a unique collaboration between the Symphonic Band and the Lafayette Ballet took place in April 2003.

Most arrive wondering what kind of talent they will find at a school with no music majors, but they leave smiling. "I'm still a bit overwhelmed," Philip Sparke wrote to Gephart after serving as a guest conductor in April 2008. "Not by the workload but by the impressive set up you have at Purdue. I'm really impressed and convinced that the bands you have are doing it for all the right reasons. Music is there to be enjoyed and it's clear all your students do that!!"

For the music department's 125th anniversary in 2011, Steven Bryant—a three-time winner of the National Band Association's William D. Revelli Composition Award (from 2007 to 2010)—was commissioned to create a new piece, which was debuted at the Purdue Bands Showcase in April of 2011. The composition was entitled "Anthem."

In March of 2006, the Wind Ensemble (then referred to as the Symphonic Band) made its Carnegie Hall debut as the showcase band at the New York Wind Band Festival.

"Carnegie Hall is perceived as only being available to the finest professionals in the world, so, in a sense, it legitimizes what we do at Purdue and what amateur musicians are able to accomplish," Gephart said. "The prestige of being selected elevates the Symphonic Band to a high level and makes everyone realize how respected it is."

It was the final performance for Bill Kisinger, who ended a thirty-seven-year career with Purdue Bands. He performed a solo on the euphonium on the Carnegie Hall stage.

"It's impossible to describe what a thrill that was," Kisinger said. "What a way to end a career. I got there about an hour before rehearsal, walked around the stage, played, and listened to the sound reverberate. You cannot believe the sound in that hall."

When he performed, he did not think about ending a long career—second only to the length of Emrick's career in Purdue Bands.

"It was one of the hardest pieces I had ever played," Kisinger said. "I was just worried about the next note. I kept thinking, 'don't screw it up.'"

He performed well and received a standing ovation.

The jazz program at Purdue represents another area of excellence in the department. Under the direction of J. Richard Dunscomb, who served as director of bands from 1981 to 1988, the jazz program experienced unprecedented growth.

When he arrived at Purdue in 1974, Dunscomb worked as an assistant with the marching band, but jazz was his first musical love. He was recruited to West Lafayette to improve the jazz programs. Jazz bands were growing at universities all across the country, but there had been no tradition of jazz at Purdue.

Purdue had a Variety Band when Dunscomb arrived, and that band played both jazz and show tunes. Eventually, the Variety Band split into the Show Band and the Jazz Band.

The first year that Dunscomb held tryouts for the Jazz Band, he had just enough applicants to fill one group—

Variety Band

Known for its singers and dancers, the Variety Band played both jazz and show tunes.

Clockwise from top left:

Robert McEmber (far right) prepares to take his Variety Band on a European Tour in 1958.

Variety Band with genies.

When Bill Kisinger started American Music Review, it had a multitude of singers and dancers. The group would narrow to a handful of singers in the 1990s.

Left: "Jazz on the Hill" has been a spring tradition since the 1970s.

Right: Female singers evoking the famous Andrews Sisters appear regularly in American Music Repertory Ensemble concerts.

seventeen. By the mid-1980s, two hundred to two hundred fifty students were trying out for the jazz program each year, and Dunscomb had three jazz bands—the Purdue Jazz Band, the Lab Jazz Band, and the Concert Jazz Band.

In addition to other expanding programs, the Variety Band continued to evolve. Going back to the 1950s, the Variety Band was doing just what its name implied, a variety of things—including jazz and dance numbers. There were singers in the group, and they presented some elaborate shows, including USO tours of Europe. In the 1970s when the jazz program broke away, the Variety Band functioned as a dance band.

When Dunscomb became director of bands in 1981, he asked Kisinger to take over the Variety Band. Kisinger was interested, but he wanted the group to explore a slightly different direction. He researched what was popular among dance bands and visited theme parks to see what was being done.

"They were doing high-energy, fast-paced performances that kept people's attention," Kisinger commented. "I said, 'That's the direction I'd like to go.'"

The American Music Review was born with an emphasis on swing-era music. By the mid-1980s, the American Music Review under Kisinger had evolved to using fourteen singer-dancers in addition to musicians.

In 1990 Jazz Band Director Lissa Fleming May started the Purdue Jazz Festival, which has become one of the largest events of its kind in the nation. This three-day jazz festival attracts nearly one hundred high school and middle school big bands and combos from throughout the Midwest to its competitions. The Jazz Festival also includes two concerts with national headliners and a variety of community events.

Among the many guest artists to appear with the Purdue Jazz Band have been Bill Watrous, Freddie Hubbard, Eddie Daniels, Tom Harrell, Howie Smith, Denis DeBlasio, Ed Shaughnessy, Marvin Stamm, Cecil Bridgewater, Gary Burton,

Formal portrait of the Purdue Symphonic Band on Carnegie Hall stage in March 2006.

Symphonic Band members pose in Times Square before Carnegie Hall debut, March 2006.

J. Richard Dunscomb (center) created a high profile for Purdue's jazz bands in the 1980s.

Allen Vizzutti, Chris Vadala, Howard Levy, Conrad Herwig, Terell Stafford, Mark Colby, Jim Pugh, Ingrid Jensen, Teri Lyne Carrington, James Williams, Bob Mintzer, Michael Philip Mossman, Wayne Bergeron, Bobby Watson, Steve Wiest, Claudio Roditi, Byron Stripling, Dave Samuels, Steve Houghton, Eric Marienthal, Bob Lark, Gary Smulyan, Dave Pietro, and Michael Weiss.

To celebrate the 125th anniversary of Purdue University Bands, the department commissioned Indiana's most prominent twenty-first century jazz composer, Brent Wallarab, to create a piece to debut at the 2011 Jazz Festival. It was titled "Kilgore's Kin."

Since 1996 the jazz studies program has been directed by M. T. "Mo" Trout. As the premier ensemble, the Purdue Jazz Band boasts a rich tradition of performing with some of the top artists in jazz today. The band travels extensively each year and has performed at many major jazz festivals and venues.

In May 2008, Trout took his jazz musicians to Europe as part of Purdue Bands' first study abroad project, "Jazz in Italy." The musicians spent two weeks studying the culture and jazz of Italy and performing at various venues around the country. The second study abroad project, in May 2011, offered an opportunity for a Purdue Jazz Ensemble to travel with the Purdue Philharmonic Orchestra and concertize in the major cities of Eastern Europe—Krakow, Vienna, Budapest, and Prague.

Having twice performed at the Montreux Jazz Festival in Switzerland, most recently in 2000, the Purdue Jazz Band has received numerous awards at festivals in the United States and abroad.

Purdue Jazz Band in Boilermaker Special, 1979.

Symphonic Band on Elliott stage during the Al Wright era.

And All that Jazz

Lab Jazz Band under the direction of graduate assistant Todd Ward, 2009–2010.

Facing page, clockwise from left:

Swing Dance at Elliott allows dancing to live jazz that is popular with students, pictured here in the early 2000s.

Caitlin Cotten sings with Purdue Jazz Band at Holiday Cheer concert in 2009.

Purdue Bands began cosponsoring Tuba Christmas, a community event, in the 2000s.

CAROLS

Montreux Jazz Festival

Purdue has played at the Montreux Jazz festival in Switzerland twice, most recently in 2000.

Clockwise from top right:

Purdue Jazz Band in front of a Swiss Alps vista.

Director M.T. "Mo" Trout and Chicago soloist Mark Colby try to fill some big shoes in The Netherlands.

Alto soloist Joe Winters.

Top: Saxophonist Eric Marienthal headlines at Purdue Jazz Festival in 2008.

Bottom: Award-winning student soloist Jason Wu plays Gershwin's "Rhapsody in Blue" with orchestra in December 2009.

Under Trout's leadership the band was selected to perform at the prestigious North Texas Jazz Festival in Dallas in 2005, and the group made a major ten-day concert tour to California in the spring of 1999. It has also been featured at the Midwest International Band and Orchestra Clinic, the Montreux-Detroit Jazz Festival, the Music Educators National Conference, and the Notre Dame Collegiate Jazz Festival. Every year the band competes at the Elmhurst College Jazz Festival, held in Chicago, and the group brings home a handful of individual awards.

An instrumental music department at a world-class university would not be complete without a symphony orchestra program. Dating back to the early twentieth century, there were orchestras operating in the Purdue Bands Department at various times under Emrick. There was even a Ukulele Orchestra that performed in Fowler Hall on October 18, 1917. During the 1930s, Emrick conducted a small pit orchestra for Harlequin shows on campus.

However, orchestras at Purdue really had their start in the Purdue Musical Organizations, accompanying singers for variety shows.

Al Wright took over as director of bands in 1954, and he started an orchestra program in late 1971 with a group called the Purdue Symphonette. It was a small group that served, among other things, as a pit orchestra for musicals. The group grew, and in 1974 it became the Purdue Symphony Orchestra, with Wright as its conductor.

Wright had no problems finding orchestra musicians for his band department. He encouraged everyone who could play a string instrument to try out. If they showed any promise, he took them, and in that way he got the program going and kept it going. "We were wall-to-wall strings, and strings

Harry Begian, Symphonic Band director in the mid-1980s, brought a national reputation to Purdue. Pictured here, he conducts a concert celebrating the Purdue Bands Department's centennial in 1986 by premiering Alfred Reed's "Praise Jerusalem!"

Orchestral Highlights

Andrew King joined Purdue faculty in 2006 as orchestra conductor and expanded the program to include two orchestras— Purdue Philharmonic and Purdue Symphony.

Facing page, clockwise from top left:

Symphonic Band members, 2000s.

David Leppla directs the Purdue Concert Band at the Long Center in downtown Lafayette during the early 2000s.

Violinist with Purdue Orchestra during the 2000s.

Ishbah Cox directs Concert Band, late 2000s.

Concert Band musicians, 2000s.

The Symphonic Band gave several concerts in the 2000s at Indianapolis' Hilbert Circle Theatre, this one featuring Broadway singer Doug LaBrecque.

are hard to get," Wright said. "We weren't as good as the Chicago Symphony Orchestra, but we were bigger."

After Wright, the orchestra was directed by Frank Stubbs and Joe Manfredo. Gephart took over in 1995 and passed the baton to Andrew King when he became director of bands in 2006.

"When I arrived at Purdue, my goal was to give a face to the orchestra," Gephart said. "There were a lot of people on and off the campus that didn't even realize we had an orchestra. We needed to create an identity."

With a full complement of strings, winds, and percussion, Purdue's orchestra tackled everything from movie themes to the most serious classical works.

One of its most anticipated events each year is the Halloween family pops concert called "Creepy Classics," with the musicians dressed in costumes.

During the administration of Purdue President Martin Jischke, the orchestra collaborated with the Purdue Musical Organizations in performances at the Hilbert Circle Theater, the home of the Indianapolis Symphony Orchestra. These performances were given in support of the University's Science Bound program.

Soloists for the Hilbert Circle Theatre concert series have included Susan Rider, trumpet/cornet, "The President's Own" United States Marine Band; Daniel Rodríguez, America's "Singing Policeman," whose career as a performer began following events of September 11, 2001; Doug LaBreque, Broadway's "Phantom of the Opera"; and Byron Stripling, jazz trumpet legend and Broadway's "Satchmo."

"Soloing with the Purdue Orchestra at the Circle Theatre was an exciting experience for me—the ensemble played with a lot of emotion and spirit," said Rider, whose performance began the series in 2003. "I truly enjoyed my time with them as I saw how the high quality of each orchestra member's character is reflected in their musical performance."

Some Purdue band programs are open to community, faculty, and staff members. One of the most known community members to take part in this opportunity was Lenore Edwards, who retired from the program in 2005 at the age of ninety-seven. She played the viola.

"She was a fixture in the orchestra," Gephart said. "The students would go to lunch with her and many still stayed in contact years later."

Another was Galen King, a professor of mechanical engineering and a bassoonist. "When we traveled he would tutor our engineering students," Gephart said.

In 1997 Purdue Bands launched a chamber music program. Pamina Blum, a renowned flutist, was the wife of a

Percussion Theater

Annual spring concerts presented by the Purdue Percussion Theater have become known for creativity in the first decade of the twenty-first century, from costumes to fireworks, from whacky works for percussion to classical pieces.

Creepy Classics

Jay Gephart introduced the idea of a Halloween orchestra pops concert for families in October 2003. It instantly became a tradition with both orchestra members and attending children dressing in costumes.

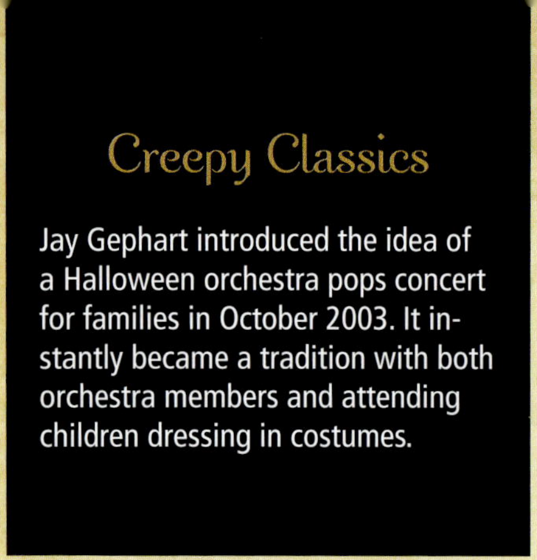

Maxine Lefever, percussion specialist and benefactor.

member of the Purdue faculty, and she advocated strongly for the program.

"We decided we would try [the chamber music program], and it was a huge success," Gephart said.

Percussion doesn't just serve as the heartbeat of the "All-American" Marching Band; it is part of every ensemble in the department. Purdue Bands also offers ensembles specifically for percussion players. Each spring the Purdue Percussion Theater presents a concert that incorporates theatrical effects with performances by the Percussion Ensemble and the Winter Drum Line.

Purdue percussion has benefited enormously from the generosity of Maxine Lefever. Lefever was a legendary figure in percussion at Purdue Bands, and "her name is synonymous with percussion education," Gephart said.

Lefever joined the staff of Purdue University 1962 and was named a professor emerita following her retirement in 1987. She died on June 20, 2004, leaving a planned gift that, among many benefits, provides new marching percussion instruments every five years.

Purdue pep bands are always on hand to keep Boilermaker spirits high at all women's and men's home basketball games as well as women's volleyball games.

The Boiler Box Band brings their unique enthusiasm to all women's home volleyball matches. Beginning in late fall and extending into early spring, two basketball bands are in high gear on campus. Boiler Brass is affiliated with the men's basketball program and Gold and Black Sound with women's basketball.

Gephart said he has an incredible faculty to lead the program. In 2011 Purdue Bands and Orchestras faculty included M. T. "Mo" Trout, jazz bands; Andrew King, orchestras; Pamela J. Nave, percussion, marching, concert, and pep bands; Max Jones, marching, concert, and pep bands; Ishbah Cox, marching, concert, brass choir, and pep bands; and Alisha Kuckartz, auxiliary director.

"We have an amazing group of professionals," he said. "What makes the whole department successful is that our faculty understands our mission. Every faculty member embraces the mission and our kids know it. We care about the success of our bands, we care about our students' academic success, and the overall experience they have at Purdue. Our mission is to help our students succeed."

At the 125 year mark of Purdue Bands and Orchestras, its organizations include the "All-American" Marching Band, two orchestras, four jazz bands, a wind ensemble, five concert bands, three pep bands, a brass choir, chamber music, and percussion ensembles.

CHAPTER NINE

TAKING IT ON THE ROAD

Band Travels on Four Continents

Standing near 77th Street and Central Park West in New York City where the 2010 Macy's Thanksgiving Day Parade was forming, Purdue University Director of Bands Jay Gephart knew his students would be positioned near the front of the procession. Then he got the news.

The Purdue "All-American" Marching Band would be *the* lead unit in the parade, ahead of all the balloons, all the floats, all the other bands and marching units, and all ten thousand participants.

"A parade official told me a little before we started that the Purdue band would pace the parade," Gephart said. This is a parade that is timed to the second for television. At 11:56 a.m. Eastern Standard Time, Santa Claus had to be in Herald Square, and for that to happen, the Purdue band had to be there at 9:56 a.m., fifty-six minutes after it started the parade.

"The official said we had to do one block a minute," Gephart continued. "That's really fast. I called the band together and told them. You should have seen the look on their faces."

But they did it. In fact, they marched a little ahead of pace and had time to stop and perform for a few minutes in Times Square.

There were 3.5 million people lining the streets of New York City that day—more than half the total population of the state of Indiana. The bystanders cheered all the way as the band marched, played, and kick-stepped through New York on a 2.65-mile route leading to Herald Square where the performance would be seen by 40 million more people watching on television.

Members of the band had been awake since 1 a.m. that morning. Gephart said he can only remember two hours of sleep in the forty-hour period before the parade. They had to get up for a middle-of-the-night rehearsal with television crews at Herald Square. When it was all over, after a family-style Thanksgiving dinner and an evening watching a show at Radio City Music Hall, the band boarded buses for the return trip to West Lafayette where they were scheduled to perform at halftime of the Purdue versus Indiana University football game on Saturday.

What was the first thing they did when they arrived back on campus late Friday afternoon? They rehearsed until dark.

The Purdue band knows how to travel and play on the road. Since the time Paul Spotts Emrick took over as band director in 1905, Purdue musicians have been part of a traveling show.

Never content to confine their performances solely to the West Lafayette campus, in the earliest days band members quickly realized the fun of traveling north for the annual football game against the University of Chicago or south to Bloomington for a game against Indiana University.

The football season travel quickly spread to off-season time on the road as the band, under the direction of Emrick, traveled throughout Indiana doing programs in community halls and high schools. At times the Purdue band performed out of state, usually in Chicago at events such as A Century of Progress International Exposition, perhaps better known as the World's Fair. In addition, the band has performed every year at the Indianapolis 500 since 1919 (read more about this event in chapter seven).

Because of the large size of the band, its trips are expensive. In fact, the high cost of travel is one of the main reasons many universities hold down the size of their bands, often limiting the organizations to a maximum of one hundred members.

In 1930 the Purdue "All-American" Marching Band of 115 made three trips during the football season, all by train.

Previous page: Selita Sue Smith leads the band at at the Osaka, Japan, 1970 World Exposition concert.

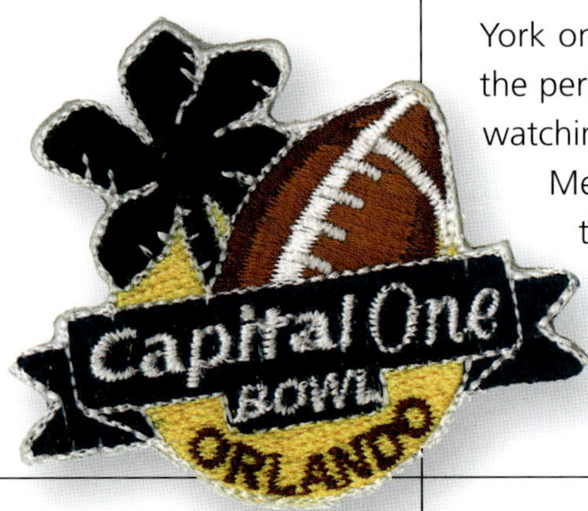

A trip to Ann Arbor for the Michigan game (the band's first trip to that location) cost $1,118; a trip to Champaign for the Illinois game cost $542; and the price of the trip to Chicago was $952.56. That came to a total of $2,612.56, no small amount in the early Great Depression years.

When Emrick asked the University administration for permission to take the band to the three games, President Edward C. Elliott wrote back stating the executive committee had voted to approve the trip to Ann Arbor.

The committee voted to defer any action as to the Purdue versus Illinois game until after the Michigan game, Elliott wrote. "Whether or not there will be any disposition to take favorable action on this will, I think, depend upon the by-products of the Michigan-Purdue game," he stated. "The members of the executive committee have noticed with growing concern the lawlessness which seems to be an inevitable accompaniment of special trains to football games at distant points. While of course it is recognized that the band is not in any way a part of such lawlessness, nevertheless, whenever the university gives permission for the band to go on such special trains it more or less places its stamp of approval on the whole affair."

Emrick's response was to let the railroads, which bid for the business of moving the band, know the executive committee's apprehension. In a letter to the railroad concerning the trip to Ann Arbor, Emrick wrote, "While there is no objection to the carrying of other passengers on this Purdue Band Special, the Wabash agrees to take due precaution against the sale of liquor on this train which might result in episodes reflecting discredit on Purdue. The Wabash agrees to provide proper officers on this special to keep the bootleggers off the trains who make it a business to accompany these excursions." This was during the Prohibition era.

Band at the Indiana State Fair in 1946.

The trip to Ann Arbor went so well that the other trips that year were approved. The admonition to the railroads carrying the band was frequently inserted at the end of Emrick's letters of agreement.

Usually band trips in those early days meant long hours of traveling. The train would leave Lafayette early in the morning, sometimes before dawn, and would return home after the game, sometimes after midnight.

The Indiana State Fair in the early part of the century was held in September, which made it easy for the band to perform at that event because school was in session and everyone was on campus.

The Block "P"

The Block "P" has been recreated by Band members and alumni in the most unlikely of places. Here is a sampling.

Clockwise from top left:

On top of Mount Fuji, 1970.

Alumni underwater in Hawaii, 2006.

In the hotel pool at the Champs Bowl, 2006.

At the Grand Canyon, 1967.

Facing page:

Band members form the Block "P" in the reflection of "The Bean" in Chicago's Millennium Park, 2011.

PURDUE
BOILERMAKERS

Right: Backstage antics at Radio City Music Hall in 1963.

"I can remember playing at the State Fair in 1921,"said Paul Hastings, class of 1922. "We played all over the fairgrounds. We divided ourselves up into three different bands and played at three different places during the day and as one big band at night. We had a great time."

Trips to Chicago often included performances in downtown theaters, parades on Michigan Avenue, and appearances at the Indiana Society of Chicago.

Orville Redenbacher, a country boy from Brazil, Indiana, who went on to cofound a popcorn empire, played in the band and maintained vivid recollections of his first trip to Chicago in 1924. The band performed that year at a party for the Indiana Society of Chicago at what was then called the Congress Hotel, today known as the Congress Plaza Hotel.

"All the important people were there," said Redenbacher in a 1986 interview. "George Ade was there. So were David Ross and John McCutcheon. That was during Prohibition, but the liquor was flowing. They had twenty-five girls there from the Chicago Academy of Music. It was an eye-opener for me. It was the first time I had ever been in a big hotel and my first experience in Chicago. I'll never forget it."

When Al Wright became director of bands in 1954, he took band travel to the next level. Where Emrick had traveled around Indiana, to away football games and events in nearby states, Wright opened the world to Purdue Bands.

Among his early opportunities was sending band members to New York City. During four summers in 1963, 1966, 1971, and 1976, members of the Purdue band played in Radio City Music Hall with the Rockettes. They were busy, but they were young and had the time of their lives.

The initial invitation came because the Purdue band had gained an excellent reputation, but Wright was never sure

exactly who recommended the organization.

He was in Atlantic City for a workshop when he received a telegram asking if he was interested in bringing a band group to New York City for the summer.

Wright actually thought the telegram was a joke.

About two weeks later, Wright received a telephone call from a Radio City Music Hall representative asking the question again. He still wasn't sure he understood. However, when the invitation came in written form, Wright was convinced, and he hurried to tell his musicians the news.

It was a tremendous coup for Wright and Purdue to have their non-music major students featured in New York City, and it helped to promote the University. It had been eight years since Purdue was featured on national radio with Paul Lavalle, and everyone was pleased with the new opportunity.

It was the chance of a lifetime for young college-age men, many from the agricultural areas of the Midwest, to live in New York City and work with the Rockettes.

"It was eleven of the best weeks any young man could ever have," said Don Daniel, a saxophonist and clarinetist from the class of 1969. He made the trip in 1966.

"To be a professional musician in Radio City at the age of twenty was an invaluable experience, and it was something I didn't really have the talent to do. I'll never forget it. We stayed at a residential hotel, and we got a waiver so we didn't have to join the union. I think after we got through paying for our room, we had about $18 a week."

What was left over was spent seeing the town.

"I was one of the more frugal ones," Daniel said. "I came home with ten or fifteen bucks and a new sport coat. We did four shows a day, seven days a week for eleven weeks. We started at 11 in the morning."

They weren't an early-to-bed, early-to-rise group. After the last show of the evening, the group went out on the town.

They also hit it off with the Rockettes. Of course, they got off to a good start. Before the group left for New York, they obtained the name of every girl in the group and sent each a red rose from the band.

"All the Rockettes were really quite friendly," Daniel said. "They didn't put us down because we were a bunch of farm boys. It turned out, most of the Rockettes were Iowa farm girls as awed with Radio City and New York as we farm boys were. And we were the first good-looking farm boys who had hit town for awhile."

DATING ON THE CHEAP

Henri Evans, who graduated in 1964 and who was on the first trip to Radio City Music Hall, said with hardly any money the band members quickly discovered the cheapest date with a Rockette—a trip to Staten Island for a hot dog and a Coke. The trip took three and a half to four hours and the total cost was $2.40. Those hours spent with a Rockette were worth $2.40 to any guy in the Purdue band, anytime.

Apparently the approach worked. Several members of the band continued dating Rockettes after they left New York, and one even married a member of the dance group!

During the second season in New York, the band members performed as if they were members of the Marine Band, and many people thought they really were Marines. The program ended with a simulated flag-raising on Iwo Jima, patriotic music, and many tearful eyes in the audience.

The special group of Purdue students had been the first college band to perform at Radio City Music Hall. The second trip in 1966 showed the reason producers were not afraid to ask Purdue to return: the opening week set a Radio City Music Hall attendance record. During 1966 more than 1.1 million people saw the show.

Under Wright, travel also became international and so extensive that students picked Purdue over other schools because of the opportunities, through the band, to visit foreign countries.

During his twenty-seven years, band trips to South America became regular events. In addition, band groups traveled to Canada, Europe, Iceland, and Japan.

Wright said it was Purdue University Vice President R. B. Stewart, in 1961, who encouraged the band to begin the journeys to South America. Stewart was the man-about-campus who got things done, and when it came to promoting the University, he never missed an opportunity. When a call came requesting that the Purdue band attend a festival with Eveready Corporation of Colombia, a division of Union Carbide, paying the tab, Stewart jumped on the chance.

With the Andes Mountains in the background, the Purdue band performs in Bolívar Square (Plaza de Bolívar) in Bogotá, Colombia in 1961. More than one million people saw the band perform on their first South American tour.

The international experience was the upside.

The downside was that the area had been so politically unstable in recent years that many bands refused to visit. Stewart approached Wright with the trip idea.

"I'll tell you what," Wright said. "We'll go, if you'll go with us." That was fine with Stewart, who also took his wife, Lillian.

Sixty-four band members made the trip, selected from a variety of University band groups, becoming, at the time, the largest Purdue instrumental ensemble to visit a foreign country.

It was an exhausting ten-day trip that included thirty appearances in twelve cities. In Colombia the band played in white ties; it marched in uniforms; it played as combos. Fifty thousand people crammed into a bullring to watch the band perform.

The band members thought they would be part of a "halftime" show in the bullring but discovered they were the whole show. Wright had to come up with routines for the band to perform as well as music for the group to play—on the spot. He did it.

Outside the bullring were another fifteen thousand people who could not get in to the venue. The band went out and played for them, too.

During the trip, more than 1 million Colombians, or one-fifteenth of the total population, heard at least one Purdue band performance. The musicians stayed in private homes during the trip and were treated like royalty.

Golden Girl June Ciampa can remember people pushing to get closer to the marching unit as it moved down the street.

"We would parade through the streets, which were really just dirt roads," she said. "People would come running out of their huts and houses and follow the parade. And then their cows would follow behind them. It was quite a parade. They would crowd around us. It was so exciting for them. They would kneel down next to us, and it would embarrass us. One time I got really frightened. I was swarmed by fifty Colombians. They were grabbing at me, and the bus was nearby, and I literally jumped over them to get to the bus."

Cars were offered for Stewart to ride in, but he insisted on marching with the band. Wherever they went, Stewart presented the local mayor with a band record album, and the albums became status symbols in the country.

At the conclusion of the tour, Fulton Freeman, the U.S. ambassador to Colombia, sent Purdue President Frederick Hovde a letter. He wrote:

Golden Girl June Ciampa signs autographs for Colombian women, 1961.

It was mainly with the little man in Colombia that the music of the band and the spirit of its individual members made such strong and enduring contact. It was with the people of Colombia in the sense of the students, the "campesinos," the taxi drivers, the small shopkeepers and others, that the communication represented by the Purdue Band was so thoroughly established. All of us will never forget this fine organization and the wonderful spirit that enabled it to complete its arduous tour with such a warm response and complete success.

HAIR "RAZING"

During a parade in South America, word filtered its way to the front of the procession that there was a problem at the back. Al Wright walked to the end of the group and asked a trumpet player about the problem.

"This guy's trying to set my hair on fire," the musician said, pointing to a man with matches. Wright knew a little Spanish. "Qué pasa? What are you doing?" he asked the young man.

It turned out the man was worried about the trumpet player being able to read music in the dark, so the man was trying to provide some light.

Majorette looks at a South American poster.

Of course, one reason that the band was never forgotten in South America was that it kept returning, performing in courtyards, concert stages, and bullrings. There would be eleven trips to South America during Wright's tenure. The students were often responsible for getting to Miami on their own, and from there, all expenses were paid from private sources in the communities in which the band performed.

Bill Kisinger, an assistant band director, can remember one year marching in a parade in South America with fireworks ignited so close to the band that the still-burning embers were falling on the members' uniforms.

In 1967 a select group of sixty-five band members headed back to Venezuela to help dedicate a bullring. The band often performed in the streets where poor people lived.

"You could go into any town and hit five notes, and you would instantly have an audience of thousands of people smiling, enjoying the Americans," Kisinger said. "A lawyer from Venezuela wrote us and said we had done more for a town where we played than the Peace Corps."

Daniel, who performed at the Radio City Music Hall, was also on the 1967 trip to Venezuela. "We were treated like visiting royalty," he said. "Every day we had four or five or six places to go. We'd play for kids and then get swarmed by kids asking for our autographs. One night, in a bar, a guy rode in on a horse, ordered a beer, sat on the horse and drank it and then rode out."

In the summer of 1970, the band travel took a big turn, from the dirt roads of South America to the Japanese World Exposition, held in Osaka.

In all, it was a three-week concert tour of Japan as guests of the Yamaha Music Foundation. One hundred and two students attended the tour. It cost them $35 each.

The Purdue band was one of only nine American cultural groups to perform at the Japanese World Exposition. Other cities that were part of the tour included Tokyo, Yokohama, Hamamatsu, Hiroshima, and Nagoya.

According to press clippings that followed their return to the United States, the Japanese were not only impressed with the musical and marching abilities of the people from Purdue, they were also impressed at the speed at which some of them could eat ice cream.

Olé!

South America was a favorite destination and Purdue Bands traveled there often.

Clockwise from top left:

"El magnifico," otherwise known as a drum major, is victorious over "el toro," a tuba player, in a scene played out in every Venezuelan bullring performance.

Drum Major David Grevenkamp surrounded by autograph seekers in Venezuela in band's last tour there in 1998.

When South Americans hold signs like this, it's no wonder the Purdue band traveled south so many times in its history.

Band during the group's trip to Japan in 1984.

More than two million people in Japan attended concerts and parades featuring the Purdue band. About two hundred thousand people were at one performance near the slopes of Mount Fuji. Later, a small group of band members climbed to the top of Mount Fuji and had a photo taken of themselves in the Block "P" formation.

In 1974 a Purdue band group went to the World Music Concert Festival in Kerkrade, Netherlands, where they performed along with the Amsterdam Concertgebouw Orchestra, the Paris Garde Republicaine Band, and the Munich Symphony Orchestra. Also in 1974 a Variety Band group led by Roger Heath put together a thirty-day Caribbean tour.

By January of 1976, the Banda de Purdue, as it was called, was back marching in the streets of Venezuela on its eighth tour of that country. In the summer of 1976, J. Richard Dunscomb, who would one day become the director of bands, at Purdue gathered a group to tour Europe and Iceland, playing jazz and Top Forty music.

The twirlers were also traveling, completing summer workshops around the world. There was one in Japan in the mid-1970s, and in June 1976 Girl in Black Lisa Ross and the Silver Twins were in Sweden teaching girls there to twirl the American way.

In 1979 the band took a trip to Canada for the Canadian National Exhibition, giving daily concerts there and also performing at night for the Scottish World Festival Tattoo (a "tattoo" is a British term for a military spectacle featuring music and marching).

In 1984 under Director Bill Moffit, a contingent of the Purdue "All-American" Marching Band made a trip to Japan in the middle of the football season. Moffit also created a special band show for the students who stayed behind for the football game.

The tour in Japan was to Osaka for a series of performances in connection with the Midosuji Parade, the Japanese equivalent of the Rose Bowl Parade in California.

Purdue and Kinki University band members trade caps in Osaka, 1984.

Many other Purdue band groups also were busy traveling in the 1980s.

In 1982 the Jazz Band, led by Dunscomb, toured Europe and performed as the featured college band at the Montreux Jazz Festival in Switzerland. The musicians then traveled to The Hague and performed at the North Sea Jazz Festival. The Jazz Band also made a second European tour in July 1987, performing extensively throughout Switzerland.

Kisinger's American Musical Review group made four Caribbean tours in the 1980s, performing in exchange for a reduced rate on room and board on the ship. A final farewell tour was mounted in 2006 as a salute to the retiring Kisinger.

Around the World

Clockwise from top left:

Golden Girl Linda Hughes twirls in front of a beer hall in the Netherlands, 1974.

At Carnaval de Québec in 1965, band members are greeted by mascot Bonhomme.

The Variety Band (with singers and dancers) participated in three USO tours (1969, 1972, and 1974).

The Purdue Jazz Band mounted a European tour in 2000, marking the third time the band had performed at the prestigious Montreux Jazz Festival in Switzerland. This particular band has also performed in Germany, the Netherlands, Japan, China, and has toured throughout the United States.

In May 2008, Director of Bands Jay Gephart took the Purdue "All-American" Marching Band to Beijing, China, to perform in the Meet in Beijing Arts Festival prior to the Olympic Games. While previous international trips had included about 100 band members, 275 made this trip to China.

Purdue was the first American college band invited by the Chinese government to perform in the nation.

While there, Gephart gave the band's new Silver Twins, Sara and Chellie Zou, the gift of a lifetime—a chance to make their debut performance at the Great Wall.

"I never imagined I would begin my Silver Twin experience in Beijing in front of my grandparents, in my dad's home country," said Sara. "It was unbelievably amazing."

Bottom, left: Al Reuther plays in the streets of Amsterdam while on the Purdue Jazz Band's European tour in 2000.

Top, right: Band at the foot of the Great Wall of China, 2008

Bottom, right: Giving high fives to youngsters following a concert at Beijing School, 2008.

Rose Bowl, 1967

Clockwise from top left:

The Band traveled by train to California. It took 14 cars to transport the 307 members that made the trip (plus the World's Largest Drum!)

At various train stops on the 1967 Rose Bowl trip, the train stopped for band parades, this one in sub-zero temperatures in Denver, Colorado.

Las Vegas had much better weather and was a fun stop on the journey west.

The trips to New York and opportunities for international travel were spectacular, but the Rose Bowl was the most coveted destination for band members. In the 1960s, Big Ten teams were not allowed to play in any post-season bowl game except the Rose Bowl. To get in the Rose Bowl, the football team had to win the Big Ten Championship or be runner-up or tied for first with the team that participated the previous year. (At that time, a Big Ten team could not go to the Rose Bowl in consecutive years.)

In the fall of 1966, Michigan State won the Big Ten title, but it had been to the Rose Bowl the previous January. Runner-up Purdue was picked to go.

Wright knew he would have to make the trip to Pasadena by train, so when the time came he called representatives from two competing railroads to his office at the same time.

"They came to my office and looked at each other," Wright said. "I told them if one of them gets the contract the other will get nothing. So the fair way to do this is one of you will take us out and the other will bring us home."

That worked just fine for the railroads.

The band made the trip in an entire train, fourteen cars and three engines chartered just for the band and cheerleaders, with the last baggage car reserved for the "World's Largest Drum."

Female students occupied a coach at the front of the train. That coach was followed by the band directors' Pullman car, a snack car, a domed observation car, a dining car, and *then* the male students—well separated from the women.

There were about 420 members of the band that year, and 307 made the trip. The size of the group might have seemed small to Purdue, but to everyone else, it was mammoth.

The size of the band that usually made the trip to Pasadena representing the other schools in the Big Ten Conference numbered about 108. So when it came time for budgeting, the Big Ten and Rose Bowl Committee refused to pay for Purdue's entire "world's biggest band." The additional funds for the trip came from the Purdue Athletic Department.

"You'll not forget our football team," Athletic Director Guy "Red" Mackey told *Los Angeles Times* sports editor Paul Zimmerman. "And you'll not forget our band when it spreads out over the entire gridiron."

Wright wasn't about to let the band pass halfway through the country without getting out and spreading a little "Hail Purdue" from time to time, so he arranged performances in Denver and Las Vegas on the way out.

In Las Vegas people left the hotels and casinos to come out on the street to hear the music. When something as big as the Purdue "All-American" Marching Band parades down the street, people come out to watch.

Since the gamblers came out to see the band, Wright wanted the band members to be able to go inside to see what a casino looked like, but most of them were underage. Wright asked the police if his group would be allowed in anyway, just for a short time.

"I'm coming back at 1 o'clock, and if your band members are in there at that time, I'll arrest them," a police officer said, according to Wright.

The officer and Wright both knew the band train would be pulling out of town by then and the students would be long gone.

But the first stop that December wasn't Las Vegas, it was Denver, and for a group that was heading from cold Indiana to sunny, warm southern California, they got a shock.

The temperature when they arrived in Denver was eighteen degrees below zero. It was snowing. It didn't matter if it officially was a blizzard or not; it was officially miserable.

Wright told the students that performing was strictly up to them. If they wanted to march, they could come out and join him. If they wanted to stay in the train, they could. Not one student stayed in the train; each musician lined up for the parade.

Purdue Golden Girl Valerie Brown took her spot at the head of the parade, dressed in her thin gold suit. For a coat, she wore only a light black cape to protect herself from the cold.

The group unloaded the big bass drum from the baggage car, positioned it, and the parade set off up 17th Street. Purdue alumni in Denver met the band train with a convertible car in which Wright would ride.

If people were surprised to see that the band went ahead with the parade, the band was surprised to see people willing to stand outside and watch.

It was 9 a.m. on Tuesday, December 27. The guys with the big drum took a few swings at it, and a head shattered in the cold. Golden Girl Brown went back to the train car after the march and quickly came down with bronchial pneumonia.

Wright had imagined a few things might go wrong on the trip, but he wasn't counting on breaking a head on the drum and the Golden Girl catching pneumonia.

He made a quick call to California where Mylar was made into Purdue drumheads, and he was able to arrange for a replacement to be available the minute the train arrived in Los Angeles, but there would be no time to paint the piece.

Wright knew that during the Rose Bowl Parade the television camera would film the drum on the band's right side. He made sure when parade time came, that the old drum head that was properly painted had its face to the camera while the new, dull, blank side faced the spectators on the left-hand side of the street.

The Golden Girl was a different matter and a bit harder to repair. "I have never been as sick before or since," Brown said.

However, Brown did perform—in sunny Las Vegas and again in the Rose Bowl Parade. She only marched in the Rose Bowl Parade long enough to pass the television camera, but she was at the football game, cheering and twirling as Purdue beat the University of Southern California. The Purdue band stayed in Los Angeles on the University of California, Los Angeles campus.

"They got us up at six in the morning, we had breakfast, and then we practiced," said William Hall, a member of the class of 1970 who played trombone and baritone. "We practiced a lot, but no one complained. We knew what we were there for."

In addition to preparing for the halftime show and Rose Bowl Parade, there were a number of special functions the band took part in, including a parade at Disneyland and a performance at the Hollywood Palladium—the first university band ever to play at the Palladium's annual Big Ten party.

Finally the Rose Bowl day arrived. The band members got out of bed at 3 a.m., put on their new uniforms, and departed for their day.

First they paraded, and then they went to the stadium, where Wright led them inside. Wright had been to the Rose Bowl only once, so he didn't know his way around the stadium as well as he knew his way around Ross-Ade.

He sent word back for the band to follow him, and it did. Orderly in all pursuits, the group formed a single file line with Wright at the head. It snaked its way through the crowd into the stadium, down a long corridor. Wright finally came to a gate.

"What are you doing here?" a guard asked.

"We're the Purdue band, and we're trying to get in," Wright replied.

"You're in the wrong place," the guard said. "You'll have to turn around and go back."

Wright motioned behind him, and the guard looked at a single file line of 307 students that stretched as far as he could see.

The guard opened the gate.

However, to get to the area reserved for them, the band members had to march all around the stadium, on the inside of the track, and in full view of the arriving crowd.

Wright had an idea. He sent word back that the band members should space themselves five yards apart in the single-file line. That meant the line of the band would stretch 1,535 yards, or the length of more than fifteen football fields.

In this locale, even a one hundred-piece college marching band was considered large.

The band marched into the stadium and received applause when the people first saw it coming through the gate. But the group kept coming and coming and coming and still coming. And people kept watching to see how long this would go on. Finally, the last Purdue band member marched through the gate and onto the field, and the crowd cheered.

Topping off all the publicity was a newspaper column by Jim Murray, a syndicated columnist with the *Los Angeles Times*. He wrote:

> *As a West Coaster, I'm getting good and bloody sick of the Big Ten Rose Bowl pact. Wait a minute, it's not the football teams. We can handle them. It's show business where they're clobbering us. In football we're 5 for 21. In bands we've been shut out. Never mind the Four Horsemen. It's the Four Glockenspielers we can't match.*
>
> *Take Monday's game. Purdue came out with a band that John Philip Sousa never dreamed of—plus, they had four girls in sequins, balloons, smoke bombs and more tubas than a hock shop on New Year's morning. The band had more people in it than the Washington Senators drew last season.*
>
> *I don't mean to take anything away from USC, but they looked like an Indian club act by comparison. "What's the name of that combo?" the press box's Bud Tucker asked suspiciously, as their thin, red line trickled out onto the field.*
>
> *I have given my attention to the difficulty, and I have put my finger on the trouble. These Big Ten bands and halftime acts come from sophisticated centers like Lafayette, Indiana.*
>
> *Naturally, they're way ahead of a bunch of rustics like us. I mean, all we have is Disneyland, Irving Berlin, MGM, Warner Brothers, Meredith Willson, Ella Fitzgerald, Ray Charles, Sinatra, Crosby and Andy Williams. How can we be expected to know anything about showbiz or how to put on a halftime musical?*

There was not another opportunity to go to a bowl game until Mark Herrmann arrived on campus and established himself as one of the leading passers in the country. With Herrmann as quarterback, Purdue went to three consecutive bowls—the Peach Bowl in Atlanta in 1978, the Bluebonnet Bowl in Houston in 1979, and the Liberty Bowl in Memphis in 1980.

The bowls were a little bit of fun and an awful lot of work for the members of the band who worked at least as hard as the football team to prepare for the performances.

Twirlers pose in front of the historic Rose Bowl Stadium in Pasadena, 2001.

Bowl Madness

Clockwise from top right:

Silver Twins (Wendy King and Erin Buescher) and Girl in Black (Nicole Ferree) employ "Boiler Up" fingers to find shade at Outback Bowl in 1999.

Floating through San Antonio on Spirit Barge, Alamo Bowl 1997–1998.

Arriving at the Sun Bowl in 2001, band members, including Scott Maxwell pictured here, were greeted at the El Paso airport by a mariachi band and dancers.

Facing page, clockwise from top left:

The band's energy did not flag during the many concerts held in the days leading up to the Rose Bowl.

Ready to step off at Disneyland, part of the 2001 Rose Bowl trip.

Band sees itself on giant screen at Capital One Bowl in Orlando, Florida, in 2004.

Tenors have fun on Gulf beach at Outback Bowl in 1999.

TOURNAMENT of ROSES
SABIAN

BLUE RIBBON

ORLANDO
Orlando Sentinel
OrlandoSentinel.com
Bud
OUC
SunTrust
ROSE BOWL

During the David Leppla years as director of bands, there were several trips. Leppla's first international trip with the band was back to Venezuela.

"The Vice President in Venezuela contacted us and said he wanted the band to come down," Leppla said. "He told us he had been a child the last time the band was there. He wanted to bring us back down so young children of that time could see us."

Under Leppla the band also traveled to Singapore for the Chingay Parade, a New Year's festival. These were great opportunities for students to experience other cultures, Leppla said, but in selecting international travel, he was also concerned about the cost.

"Another thing I was always concerned about was putting too much demand on students' time," he said. "We needed to keep that in perspective."

Also limiting international travel during the Leppla years was the fact that when Joe Tiller became coach of the Purdue football team, they started going to bowl games, and that involved band travel. In Tiller's twelve years at Purdue, the University went to ten bowl games.

At the end of the 2000 football season, as the clock ticked down in a victory over Indiana University in Ross-Ade Stadium, the Purdue "All-American" Marching Band started playing "California Here We Come" and "Everything's Coming Up Roses." It was the moment the crowd had anticipated.

Purdue was going back to the Rose Bowl for only the second time in its history. Of course, with the team went the band that Tiller had always praised as the spirit of Ross-Ade Stadium.

When there are thirty-four years between Rose Bowl trips, things change, and the trip west was much different for the band in 2000 than it had been in 1966.

The band flew this time, instead of taking the train. However, the students who performed on New Year's Day 2001 in the Rose Bowl Parade and at the game received the same national acclaim that followed the band thirty-four years earlier.

Coincidentally, band member Tim Head of Evansville followed in the footsteps of his father who played in the 1967 Rose Bowl band. "If you do the math, the chances of my dad being there and then having a son go back, it's phenomenal," Head wrote in a band remembrance.

Scott Maxwell called the Rose Bowl trip "the longest, hardest, and most strenuous five days of my entire life. But, damn it, we played our hearts out to support Purdue and I will remember it forever."

Leppla said some of the other bowl trips the band made allowed plenty of time for fun, but the Rose Bowl required a number of performances.

The group arrived in Los Angeles on Thursday, December 28, with temperatures in the seventies. However, the notion of going out to play in the sun quickly dissolved in a three-hour practice that lasted until 10:30 p.m. Pacific time, or 1:30 a.m. back in Indiana where they had started the day.

The opponent was the University of Washington, and on Friday, December 29, the two bands joined in a march down Main Street in Disneyland followed by some time in the park.

On Saturday, December 30, the band traveled by bus to Pasadena to tape a CBS Parade Special "Coming Up Roses." They visited a float building site and performed for fifteen thousand Boilermakers at a pep rally in Century City where attendees lined up to get their photo taken with the big bass drum. That evening the band broke up into "pep" units to play for alumni gatherings.

The next morning, Sunday, December 31, a pep band left at 8:30 a.m. to perform at a parents' reception and a kickoff luncheon. Other band members paraded to Santa Monica Pier to match musical wits with the University of Washington band.

The Purdue band performed at a New Year's Eve event that night, but it ended long before midnight. Wake up call on Monday, New Year's Day, was 4 a.m. At 8:37 a.m. the band took off on the five and a half-mile parade route down Colorado Boulevard.

"It's a very long and very grueling parade," Leppla said. "We marched all over campus that December getting everyone ready for that five and a half-mile parade."

Drum major Shaun Jones will never forget the event:

> *I remember looking back at the band during the parade and just thinking—wow! Our lines were straight, the sound was good, and the fans loved it. All along the parade route Purdue fans cheered wildly when the band broke into the fight song. It energized the marchers.*
>
> *As we turned off the boulevard, the breathtaking mountain vista that greeted us produced goose pimples and provided the perfect end to a tremendous parade performance. None of the 315 band members had to drop out along the way, but all were in a state beyond sore—numb!*

At the stadium that afternoon, there was not a moment when the band was not playing or cheering. When the game was over, the band members lined the road to cheer the team buses as they left the stadium.

"The one thing I'll never forget is the last glimpse of the field and stadium as we walked out of the Rose Bowl," said flag corps member Cassandra Gray.

"We had lost the game, but in reality, we had won just by going."

The Purdue "All-American" Marching Band, under the direction of David Leppla, performs at the January 20, 1989 Inaugural Parade for George H. W. Bush and James D. Quayle.

Purdue is the first Big Ten band in Macy's Thanksgiving Day Parade, 2010.

CHAPTER TEN

HAIL PURDUE

Previous page: Trumpeters perform the "PSP" version of "Hail Purdue," which means the group plays, sings, and plays the school song.

One of a few women to twirl as both Girl in Black and Golden Girl, Kim Ratcliffe served in total from 1986–1990.

Since 1912 every person in the "All-American" Marching Band has had one thing in common—"Hail Purdue."

The song has been played at football games, basketball games, pep rallies, and marches. It has been played from China to Venezuela. Every time something good happens to the University, people look to the band to play "Hail Purdue."

The Purdue fight song is part of the life and spirit of the University. It is the song played by members of the band more than any other piece of music.

The lyrics were written by James R. Morrison, class of 1915 and the music was the work of Edward J. Wotowa, class of 1912.

Morrison died at a young age in 1929, but Wotowa led a long, happy life and returned to Purdue for his forty-fifth class reunion in 1957. On that occasion, Al Wright, the band director at the time, handed Wotowa the baton and let him conduct the song he had composed.

Later that year, Wotowa recalled how the song came into being in an article for the *Purdue Alumnus*:

> *James Morrison wrote to me in 1912, following my graduation, saying: "We are in need of a war song, and I have, therefore, indited the following lyrics with the hope that you will set them to music in order that they might be sung in Chapel."*
>
> *Jimmie was a true poet, not just a rhymester. Jimmie's lyrics were so good that more acclaim is due him than has been given him, acclaim which he so richly deserves. In fact, his lyrics were so good that in just reading them, one would naturally "sing-song" them. Hence, it was not difficult to set them to music. After a few readings, a melody just naturally seemed to evolve. Accordingly, I made an arrangement for piano and voice and one for Male Chorus and sent them to Mr. Morrison. He, in turn, as I remember him telling, gave it to the then existing Glee Club and had it sung at Chapel where it immediately met with popular favor. Subsequently, it was adopted as the official Purdue song.*
>
> *I am thankful that it happened to be my lot to write the melody which has been so closely associated with that great Purdue spirit through the years. You can hardly read the words to the song without hearing the music. It makes you want to watch a football game.*

No doubt "Hail Purdue" met with approval from Director Paul Spotts Emrick, because little music was played at the University in those early twentieth-century days without his official endorsement. As band director from 1905 to 1954, Emrick selected the music that was played, arranged some of it, wrote some of it, and launched traditions that continue into the twenty-first century.

Al Wright came to Purdue in 1954 and immediately made exciting changes in the band. He also added many more traditions through the years. One of his most beloved traditions is the "I Am An American," which started in 1966.

That was a time of political and social unrest and campus protest, but Purdue remained relatively calm. There were demonstrations at Purdue, but nothing compared to what was happening at some other Big Ten schools and universities in the East and West.

It was during this time that Wright hit upon one of the most patriotic themes that the band would perform.

Jack Scott was the spark that ignited the idea. Scott was publisher of the *Journal and Courier* in Lafayette. He was a

HAIL PURDUE

Hail Purdue!
To your call once more we rally,
Alma Mater, hear our praise;
Where the Wabash spreads its valley,
Filled with joy our voices raise.
From the skies in swelling echoes
Come the cheers that tell the tale
Of your vic'tries and your heroes,
Hail Purdue! We sing all hail!

Chorus:
Hail, Hail to Old Purdue!
All hail to our old gold and black!
Hail, Hail to Old Purdue!
Our friendship may she never lack,
Ever grateful, every true,
Thus we raise our song anew,
Of the days we've spent with you
All hail our own Purdue!

former mayor of South Bend and a retired Marine Corps general who appreciated a good rousing band show and an open display of patriotism. Scott approached Wright with the idea for a halftime show at Ross-Ade Stadium to call attention to the patriotism of the people of Indiana.

The idea appealed to Wright, who gathered U.S. flags and had a patriotic musical arrangement created. He needed something more, however, so he went through ideas until he came up with a short speech called "I Am An American." He got the idea for the words from a message printed on the menu of a Lafayette restaurant, the Downtowner, whose owners wanted to show their patriotism. Wright's script was used in the band's patriotic show:

> *I am an American. That's the way most of us put it, just matter of factly. They are plain words, those four. You could write them on your thumbnail, or you could sweep them clear across a bright autumn sky. But remember, too, that they are more than words. They are a way of life. So whenever you speak them, speak them firmly; speak them proudly; speak them gratefully. I am an American.*

The piece was a great success, but the next week the band performed a show that was completely different, trying to meet audience demand for new and fresh material. Following the new show, an editorial appeared in Scott's *Journal and Courier* asking what had happened to the "I Am An American" speech.

So Wright decided the band would perform the piece again, and they did it at every home performance that season during the flag-raising ceremony. The next season the band put the speech behind them for a second time. People again complained that the program element should be included.

Roy A. Johnson, "Voice of the Purdue Bands," began his association with the band as a student in 1956.

THE CHEER

Hell Yes, Damn Right, You Bet, No Sweat, Gung Ho, Cha-Cha-Cha, Unhh, Samba, Bicycle, Cervesa, Scooby Dooby Doo, And All That Jazz, Roses, Yup, Bufori, El Bano, Smax, Howaya, Peaches, Reerr, Butter, Ciao, Bush, Chingay, Sudler, Alamo, Fiss, Coach, Jing, Snoopy, Awesome!

The official band cheer goes back to the 1950s. Shouted with enthusiasm on various occasions when the spirit calls, as well as during the post-game concerts, the cheer is composed of words or phrases band groups have added over the years.

The words come from bowl trips, trips to South America, or they represent a person or an attitude in the band during a given year. The lyrics give the marching band members a link to their past, to the people who marched before them:

The cheer started when cheerleaders in the stadium shouted "**Are we going to beat** . . ." and the students shouted back "**Hell yes**."

The band decided to add its own cheer, "**Hell yes, damn right**," and it went from there with various words added over the years.

"**You bet**" was an attempt to eliminate the swearing. Instead of replacing those words, however, the phrase was added to the cheer.

"**No sweat**" is what happens to the band during November games when the woolen suits feel just right after a hot September and warm October.

"**Gung ho**" is the band's constant attitude.

"**Cha-cha-cha**" comes from the 1963 trip to Radio City Music Hall.

"**Unhh**" is also from that trip.

"**Samba**" is the one word members of the band spoke during the 1963 show.

"**Bicycle**" comes from the time a male student tried to ride a bike through a band practice.

"**Cervesa**," Spanish for beer, was added when the head drummer "sold" the drum major for a round of beers during the 1963 South America trip.

"**Scooby Dooby Doo**" comes from the 1966 Radio City Musical Hall trip.

"**And all that jazz**" is also from that trip.

"**Roses**" represents the 1967 Rose Bowl.

"**Yup**" serves as a response to the question, "Do we have the best damned band in the land?"

"**Bufori**," Japanese for crab, comes from the 1970 Japanese World Exposition trip.

"**El bano**," Spanish for bathroom, references the health problems band members experienced during a trip to Venezuela in 1972.

"**Smax**" is a reminder of the time Assistant Director Maxine (Max) Lefever was smacked across the face while trying to photograph prostitutes in Amsterdam in 1974.

"**Howaya**" was the New York greeting from a Radio City Musical Hall trip in 1974.

"**Peaches**" references the Peach Bowl in 1978.

"**Reerr**" mimics the sound of bagpipes from the 1979 Canadian National Exposition trip.

"**Butter**" comes from the 1979 Houston Bluebonnet Bowl.

"**Ciao**" is from the trip to Venezuela in 1972. The chicas always said good-bye using the Italian word "Ciao" in lieu of "Adios."

"**Bush**" hails from the 1989 Inaugural Parade in Washington, D.C.

The Purdue "All-American" Marching Band, under the direction of Jay Gephart, forms a Block "P" beside the Great Wall on their 2008 trip to Beijing, China. The word "Jing" was added to the band cheer following this trip.

"**Chingay**" represents the Singapore Chingay Parade in 1992.

"**Sudler**" remembers the year 1995, when Purdue received the Sudler Trophy for Excellence in College Marching Bands. Named for the late Louis Sudler, the award is referred to by students as the "Heisman Trophy for bands." Sudler was a Chicago businessman who helped to bring about the Chicago Symphony Orchestra's return to international renown in the late 1960s and 1970s

"**Alamo**" comes from the 1997 Alamo Bowl.

"**Fiss**" is an acronym for Feria Internacional de San Sebastian where the band performed in 1974.

"**Coach**" is for Bill Kisinger. The word was added in 2005 when he retired after thirty-seven years with the band. The students called him "Coach."

"**Jing**" references the pre-Olympics trip to Beijing in 2008. Jing is used to represent the city on license plates.

"**Snoopy**" was added in 2010 when the band led the Macy's Thanksgiving Day Parade with the Snoopy balloon following right behind them.

"**Awesome**" represents what the band is, always.

Trumpeters, 1944–1945

Wright responded by reshaping the tradition, rewording the script, and substituting some different phrases. "People were incensed," he said. "You would think we had rewritten the Bible." He put the original version back in the show, and the band has used the "I Am An American" speech at every home game since and at some away games.

Sometime around the Gulf War in the early 1990s, the Purdue crowds started chiming in on the reading's last line—"I Am An American"—and that has also become a tradition.

After the terrorist attacks of September 11, 2001, Purdue Bands received requests for the words to "I Am An American" from all around the country.

Although different announcers presented "I Am An American" in the early years, the honor of presenting it since 1973 belongs to the "Voice of the Purdue Bands," Roy A. Johnson.

Johnson—a former member of the band, class of 1960, and a former assistant band director, has the opportunity to hear all the comments on the band music from the stadium pavilions where he announces the halftime shows.

The bowl game scouts, he said, are always impressed with Purdue's pre-game, halftime, and post-game shows.

One year a group from the Florida Citrus Bowl said the Purdue band was the best it had ever seen. They wished out loud that they could get the band down to Florida for the bowl game. Unfortunately, the group was at Ross-Ade Stadium that year to watch the visiting team.

Former Director of the Alumni Association Joe Rudolph said the marching band is one of the major advantages in getting Purdue into bowl games.

"When you talk with representatives from bowls, they always say, 'We'd sure like to get your band,'" Rudolph said. "We've got a good chance of being invited places because we've got an exciting football team, and we have a four hundred-plus-piece band we take with us wherever we go. The bowl representatives don't make any bones about telling us they like the band. As far as public relations go, I think the band and the Glee Club are the two greatest assets the University has, and it's not only the quality of the music that people are impressed with. They're impressed with the students themselves."

The students in the marching band have their own band cheers and traditions, many of which are part of their march out of Ross-Ade Stadium to Hovde Hall and the post-game concert. Filing out of the stadium, the band marches to a percussion cadence, cheers, and plays "Hail Purdue," "Fighting Varsity," and "For the Honor of Old Purdue."

Once the whole band is across Stadium Avenue and on the Stadium Mall, the group stops for "Tuba Cadence," a song about aching muscles accompanied by tubas.

The words change a bit from section to section depending on what part of the band members' bodies hurt the most after a long day of playing and marching, but generally the lyrics lament the pains of carrying a heavy instrument.

Oh my gosh my shoulders hurt, oh the pain.
Oh my gosh my shoulders hurt, oh the pain.
Oh my gosh my shoulders hurt, oh the pain.
I don't think I'll ever do this again.

Oh my gosh my feet hurt, oh the pain.
Oh my gosh my back hurts, oh the pain.
Oh my gosh my neck hurts, oh the pain.
I don't think I'll ever do this again . . .

Well, maybe one more time . . .

This is immediately followed by a cadence from the drum line, and the band returns to playing and marching.

Band members also have their own words for a third verse to "Hail Purdue":

In the Band we march and swagger
As we play for old Purdue.
At the halftime we do shows
No other band on Earth could do.
When we cheer the Earth will tremble,
For we're known throughout the land
As the best in marching music,
We're the Boilermaker Band!

Michael Esposito, a tuba player, reacts to action on the field during a 2001 game versus Iowa.

Next page: The band performs in Herald Square at the Macy's Thanksgiving Day Parade in 2010, an event televised around the world.

At the end of band camp one summer day, Director of Bands Jay Gephart asked the members to name the band traditions. The students came up with more than fifty in less than five minutes, and then one band member hit on a tradition that summed up all the rest. It was just one word: excellence.

As the students themselves shout, they are "the best damn band in the land."

Believe

Index

Purdue
Jazz Bands